MISSION
- AN INVITATION
TO GOD'S FUTURE

Papers read at the biennial conference of the
British and Irish Association for Mission Studies
at St Stephen's House, Oxford,
June 28 – July 1 1999.

Edited by
Timothy Yates

CLIFF COLLEGE
PUBLISHING

ISBN 1 898362 25 4
© 2000 Cliff College Publishing

British Library Cataloguing in Publication Data.
A catalogue record for this book is available
from the British Library.

**Cliff College Publishing,
Calver, Hope Valley, Nr Sheffield S32 3XG**

Printed, using data supplied on disk, by:

MOORLEY'S Print & Publishing

23 Park Rd., Ilkeston, Derbys DE7 5DA
Tel/Fax: (0115) 932 0643

CONTENTS

The British and Irish Association for Mission Studies is an inter-confessional body founded in 1990 as a forum for both academic teachers and missionary practitioners and others interested in mission.

It publishes a twice-yearly newsletter and holds day conferences and biennial residential conferences.

Details of membership can be obtained from the Secretary,
C/o The Henry Martyn Centre,
Westminster College,
Cambridge CB3 OAA
or from the website
http://www.martynmission.cam.ac.uk/BIAMSConf.htm

CONTRIBUTORS

Professor Jürgen Moltmann is Emeritus Professor of Systematic Theology in the Protestant Faculty of the University of Tübingen.

Professor Theo Sundermeier is Professor of the History of Religions and Missiology at the University of Heidelberg.

Professor Anton Wessels is Professor of Missiology and Religion at the Free University of Amsterdam and is a member of BIAMS.

Professor Christopher Rowland is Dean Ireland's Professor of Exegesis of Holy Scripture in the University of Oxford.

The Revd Jane Grinonneau is a Baptist minister from Sheffield.

The Revd Julia Dowling is a Methodist minister from Luton.

The Revd Dr Philip Thomas is an Anglican incumbent in the diocese of Durham and co-ordinator of the BIAMS special interest groups.

Kirsteen Kim is secretary of the Henry Martyn Centre in Cambridge, a doctoral student of the University of Birmingham and secretary of BIAMS.

Dr David Smith is co-ordinator of the Whitefield Institute in Oxford.

Dr John d'Arcy May teaches in the Irish School of Ecumenics in Dublin and is a member of BIAMS.

The Revd Canon Timothy Yates is a canon of Derby Cathedral and editor of the BIAMS newsletter.

PREFACE

The British and Irish Association for Mission Studies is a comparative newcomer to the academic and theological scene. It was founded in 1990 and held its inaugural meeting in Edinburgh (July 9-12, 1990) at a conference which in part recalled the great Edinburgh meeting of 1910, convened by Professor Andrew Walls and entitled 'New Prospects for Mission'. Since then regular biennial residential conferences have been interspersed with day conferences. The papers which follow were all delivered at the conference of 1999, held at St Stephen's House, Oxford under the title 'Mission – an invitation to God's future'. In his welcome to the University of Oxford, Professor Christopher Rowland drew attention to the Apocalypse in relation to the title: here was thinking about millennium which had a subversive approach to all world authority, echoed in the writings of the nineteenth century poet and Christian visionary, William Blake. Professor Jürgen Moltmann delivered an invigorating theological vision, which emphasised that Christianity was about life and that its mission in the 21st Century would be about enhanced life for people and nations. In successive papers, Europe and the West became the focus: Professor Theo Sundermeier analysed its pluralism and 'bricolage-religiousness', while Professor Anton Wessels addressed its secularity and how far the use of great visual artists like van Gogh and Chagall and its poets could serve to introduce sacred moments or signals of transcendence to such a culture. In the contributions which followed, the report of a meeting of European missiologists at Stavangar explored the phenomena of Islam and New Religious Movements in Europe; case studies of urban settings in Sheffield and Luton exposed European secularism and pluralism in their sharpest form and a Christian presence and witness which had been re-shaped in response to context; David Smith's bleak but realistic paper described Christianity's apparently terminal decline in the West; issues of post-modernity in relation to the work of David Bosch were handled by Kirsteen Kim; and, after the conference ended, a helpful post-logue and stimulating exchange on its contents took place between two participants, Philip Thomas and John d' Arcy May.

It is hoped that this body of material will be of interest and help to all who grapple with mission in the West and not only members of the association. The BIAMS executive wish to place on record their debt to the contributors, to their hosts at St Stephen's House and especially to the Revd. Andrew Burnham, its vice-principal; and most particularly, to the principal, the Revd. Howard Mellor and the publishing arm of Cliff College, Calver, now an important resource for mission studies as a constituent college of the University of Sheffield, who have made this publication possible.

Fr. Danilo Castello (chairman) on behalf of BIAMS

Timothy Yates (editor)

Introduction

'A community which hears the Apocalypse'

Christopher Rowland

I teach in a university whose theology is dominated by a historical theological orientation. This has many strengths as well as shortcomings. Among its strengths is the availability it offers to our students to consider the wide exemplifications of the Christian theological task, not least of which is the mission of the church, which could well be viewed from the perspective of mission. It is a pressing question. Recently the Diocese of Oxford discussed the need to give priority to mission and discipleship. I am aware that the unequivocal commitment to themes of God's kingdom and the needs of the world sit uneasily with the mission of the church bequeathed by Christendom with its buildings of exquisite beauty and patterns of worship and ministry rooted in an earlier part of this millennium. How the theme of this conference fits in with mission is not immediately apparent until one looks at a text like Ephesians where the ministry of the church is to proclaim to the whole of creation, including the principalities and powers, the counsel of God. The proclamation of the eternal gospel in the Apocalypse is one which is always ambiguous, involving the offer of grace at the same time as the moment of crisis. The apostle Paul too includes in the gospel the revelation of God's justice and the revelation of God's wrath (Rom 1: 16f). It is a juxtaposition which is very much akin to the revelation of God's salvation and judgement as interlocking manifestations of the divine purpose, in Revelation.[1] As in Revelation so in Rom 1, the wrath mentioned is God's eschatological wrath manifested against impiety and injustice, particularly evident in idolatry. Idolatrous behaviour leads to a perverted outlook on the world, and a failure to recognise the ways and acts of God (cf. Rev 9:20). Idolatry is a

---

1   See further G. Bornkamm 'The Revelation of God's wrath', in *Early Christian Experience* (London, SCM, 1969) pp. 47ff

social as well as spiritual evil, promoting patterns of life which depart from the exercise of the justice and mercy of God. What we are offered in Romans 1, is a more prosaic description of a world marked by deceit and human selfishness, stripped of the apocalyptic symbolism of Rev 6: 8-9.

For today's introductory talk, I thought I would try to offer a perspective which is rooted in my own theological research interests. I think that I can best summarise that perspective by quoting the following words of Dietrich Bonhoeffer:

the church must be a community which hears the Apocalypse and testifies to its alien nature and resists the false principle of inner worldliness[2]

There are three points to which I wish to draw your attention:

- hearing the Apocalypse
- alien nature
- resisting worldliness

I want to explore what it might be to be a church of the Apocalypse by looking at the Apocalypse itself and a major interpreter of it. We need to hear the Apocalypse. It is a religious outlook and practice which is unpredictable and challenging, not beloved by those who long for order and stability. Apocalypticism in Judaism and Christianity is rooted in perception of the divine purpose in the manifestation of divine knowledge through revelation by vision, audition or dream. This knowledge includes anything concerning human destiny and the nature of divine purposes, whether of the past, present or the future and could extend to knowledge of the divinity and the heavenly world (this is particularly the case with the Jewish apocalyptic and mystical tradition). The importance of apocalypticism may be demonstrated by the appearance of a major encyclopaedic survey of the phenomenon in world religion.[3]

---

2   D. Bonhoeffer, *No Rusty Swords* (London, 1965) pp 324-5

3   *The Encyclopedia of Apocalypticism Volume 1 The Origins of Apocalypticism in Judaism and Christianity*, edited by John J. Collins, *The Encyclopedia of Apocalypticism Volume 2 Apocalypticism in Western History and Culture*, edited by Bernard McGinn, *The Encyclopedia of Apocalypticism Volume 3 Apocalypticism in the Modern Period and the Contemporary Age* edited Stephen J. Stein (New York, Continuum,1998).

In contemporary Christianity the privileged status presupposed by apocalyptic revelation can be found in contrasting wings of Christian faith and practice. On the one hand the apocalyptic literature of the Bible has proved to be a fertile ground for understandings of the Christian mission. Thus, in contemporary Christianity committed to pre-millennialism, a particular sketch of biblical eschatology based on Daniel, Ezekiel, Revelation and 1 Thessalonians offers a scenario in which the world is destined to inevitable destruction, while the elect are safeguarded by their divine removal through the Rapture. In view of that prospect, the only safe place is to be born again and thereby guarantee an escape from the terrors of the end-time. In the light of this, the most appropriate course of action is to engage in a mission which will draw as many as possible into that privileged circle and leave a corrupt world to spin inexorably to its foreordained destruction.

An apocalyptic theology influenced by liberationist hermeneutics, on the other hand, holds the view that the perspective of the poor must be determinative of the mission of the church. It is with them that God is particularly present; and action done to and with them is activity directed towards God. In other respects, also, liberation theology draws on the theological perspective of the apocalyptic tradition: reading the signs of the times, the critique of ideology and prophetic theology. In examining the role of apocalypse in determining mission we saw how often a sense of certainty undergirded courses of action.

The prophetic critique of social arrangements can be done via a mixture of Christian insight and socio-economic analysis. That assessment, however sophisticated, is supported by the view that insight into the true nature of history and institutions is a present possibility. In recent years in South Africa the writers of the *Kairos* document have attempted to practise the wisdom of apocalypse and read the signs of the times by offering a searching critique of state manipulation of religion and politically anodyne trends in theology. There is then the need for an outspoken prophetic theology which criticizes the status quo from the perspective of the oppressed, and, thereby, engages in action to bring about moves to justice.[4] For the *Kairos* theologians to be a church of the Apocalypse is of the essence of the church's mission. We too need to be reminded that there is an apocalyptic language

---

4   The Kairos Document (London, CIIR, 1985)

rooted in Daniel and Ezekiel which served generations of prophets and seers in Judaism and Christianity as they sought to see the ways of God's justice and judgement in the world in which they lived. This apocalyptic discourse beckons us do more than analyse and organise its images; rather to be open, to be influenced and challenged by them as we would by a piece of music, painting or particularly poignant situation.[5]

The marking of the Millennium is a wider context of this conference. The focus of the Millennium celebrations in these islands is the Millennium Dome on the bank of the Thames. Despite its apocalyptic sounding title, there seems little of the Apocalypse in that edifice. Yet the lack of an apocalyptic edge is also (more surprisingly) evident in the church discussions of the Millennium. One would hardly guess that Revelation 20 had anything to offer to the marking of the Millennium, but the secular Dome organisers may have stolen a march on their ecclesiastical peers. I heard from a friend that William Blake was to be the poet of the Millennium. No-one has understood the Apocalypse better than Blake. Yet, perhaps predictably, Blake's contribution to the Dome may well end up being a couple of Songs of Innocence and Experience and Jerusalem, the latter words taken out of context,[6] of course, sung by heavenly-sounding choirs, thereby managing to domesticate the great prophet against empire, and its lackey, religion. One wonders whether the choice of Blake is another example of building the tombs of the prophets after their deaths and not recognising the prophetic spirit at work in our midst, warning and encouraging the down-hearted, in the persons of the ecoprophets of doom and the poor and the dispossessed, who are themselves finding their voices.

William Blake was one who turned to the Apocalypse as a text offering him the language to interpret the brutal realities of his day: oppressive monarchy; state power; violence; all aided by a compliant ecclesiastical control and subservient theology. In 1799 he scrawled in the margin of one of his books 'the Beast and Babylon rule without control'. He used the Apocalypse as a lens through which to discern the reality of things which are happening,

---

5   For a reading or Revelation which attends to this dimension in the history of interpretation and in contemporary practice, see C. Rowland, *Revelation New Interpreter's Bible*, vol xii (Nashville, Abingdon, 1998).
6   They are found in one version of Blake's poem 'Milton' as a prologue.

to read the signs of his times. It offered a way of reading the world and a tool to combat human ill/de-lusion. To quote the words of William Stringfellow who uses the Apocalypse in a way similar to Blake:

> Revelation is a parable of the fallenness of nations - a means of seeing things differently. It offers a converted sense of time, a transposed perception of history. In the same event one may discern the moral reality of death and there is the incarnation of the Word of God, the demonic and the dehumanising and the power of the resurrection, the portents of the Apocalypse impending and the signs of the imminence of the Eschaton. Apocalypse is more a question of offering reorientation. It impends upon each and every happening. Babylon a description of every city, an allegory of the condition of death. Jerusalem is about the emancipation of human life in society from the rule of death, the message of a prophetic church, which offers an anticipation of the end of time. The Christian exposes the reign of death while affirming the aspiration to new life, an exemplary human being, a mature and free person; a humanised human being; a prophet is one whose work is intercession for human life the faithful public advocacy of human life in society, the proclamation and provocation of redemption[7]

Blake understood the political, spiritual and economic forces at work in late eighteenth-early nineteenth centuries which led to the domestication of true religion. He also recognised the difficulty of the prophet's role: the isolation and the necessity for a long, hard task of changing the way in which people view their world - hence the illuminated books. He was a forerunner of contemporary liberation theology; reading the signs of the times; himself always living on the edge of subsistence; with an intimate insight into the exploitation of the poor and the ease with which rich and poor alike are led astray by the delusion of a dominant ideology. His is an extraordinary wisdom from outside the academy. For Blake, open to the wisdom of God from a variety of quarters, the Spirit had been truly poured out on all flesh and he expected to find marks of its activity in diverse persons and places. He could see the importance of the voice of the outcast and the marginal (nowhere better exemplified than in the way in which he gives the 'Little Black Boy' a voice in the poem of that name in 'Songs of Innocence'). He articulates the value of his own experience over against a dominant Christian ideology which is in danger of

---

7   W. Stringfellow *Ethic for Christians and Other Aliens in a Strange Land* (Waco, 1977)

forgetting its alternative and counter-cultural position, bearing witness to the future reign of God on earth.

It takes another Christian eccentric rebel to recognise the importance of what Blake was doing and the challenge he posed to the Christian church of his day. Alan Ecclestone,[8] scholar, inner city priest, and communist wrote as follows of Blake and the way in which he exposed the subtle corruptions of the gospel that went on in the life of the church:

> Blake found men and women using the Bible in the very way Christ had deplored, because they had ceased to learn to speak in the Spirit in their own tongues. They were as those who laboriously learned a dead language and made it the tomb of the Spirit.... Blake was shaping a new language to express a conception of human life, of incarnate love, of the triumph of Christ, of body and spirit made one flesh, for which there were no adequate images in the minds of men and women in his time. Such imagery has to be new-made over and over again. Only so can the old imagery be reborn, only so can Scripture and the spiritual experiences of human beings of other generations become present truth and quickening words.[9]

It is strange that the imminence of the millennium should provoke a debate about appropriate ways of celebrating it. The usual emphasis in most British church contexts is on the millennium as a commemoration of the Incarnation (perhaps we need to remind ourselves that in the Gospel of John the incarnation is about a crisis and there is no easy baptising of the status quo.) I find all this bizarre when we consider such proposals in the light of the text which has led to millenarian beliefs, Revelation 20. Far from the world enjoying a celebration to mark the millennium, this chapter reminds us that we stand under the judgement of God and faced with the rule of those whose lives had been taken over by a society which rejoiced to see the death of those who tormented it with their witness to God's justice (Rev. 11. 10). This passage looks forward to a period when the messianic reign would take place on earth. It is a fulfilment then of the prayer of Jesus: 'thy kingdom come, thy will be done *on earth* as it is in heaven'. Those who reign have shown themselves fit to do so because they are the ones who have identified themselves with the way of the Lamb, even at the cost of their lives. They are peculiarly qualified because of their espousal of another form of governance

---

8   T. Gorringe *Alan Ecclestone: Priest as Revolutionary* (Sheffield, 1994)
9   A. Ecclestone *Yes to God* (London, 1975).

(paralleled in the words of Jesus in Mark 10:42f).[10] It is those whose life follows in the footsteps of the Messiah, refusing to accept the injustice of the old order and holding out for something different, who can truly represent humanity to God and God to humanity as priests. The millennium is an age which will be marked by that alternative pattern of life which had been followed by a minority, yet ridiculed, in the old order. Their style of life is now seen to be relevant and applicable.

Another major theme of the book of Revelation is the resistance necessary against the beast and Babylon in the light of the disclosure that the Lamb who was slain is the Messiah. The emergence of this loser and insignificant one provokes a massive upheaval and crisis in the culture of the Beast and Babylon, which cannot continue to exist in the face of this new way. In Revelation 4, John sees God lauded in heaven in a vision which utilises the images of Ezekiel, Isaiah and Daniel. The acknowledgement of the divine creator by the heavenly host contrasts with the rebellion and disorder on earth. What we have in the various visions is a movement from heaven to earth, when the new Jerusalem comes down from heaven and the divine tabernacling is with people in chs.21-22, when the division between heaven and earth is overcome. The vision of the slaughtered lamb's place with God reminds us that the gospel offers an alternative story. The vindication of the Lamb who was slain provokes a violent crisis, as is evident from the visions which follow in Rev 6. The revelation of the gospel reveals a world dominated by injustice and full of violence.

In the midst of the chaos of a disordered world, which John sees in a new light as the result of his vision, he is called to prophesy (Ch. 10). And, shown in a vision, is the kind of prophetic witness that is expected in the midst of ordinary life. For churches tempted to compromise with the life of Babylon, it has become necessary to recall them to their vocation. This witness is directed against the all-encompassing demands of empire. In Rev. 13 passages from Daniel and Revelation offer a potent insight into the nature of state power and the need for vigilance on the part of the people of God in the face of the persuasiveness of its plausible might. We are offered in Revelation 13 & 17 a graphic portrait of the nature and operation of ideology, which creates support, and,

---

10   K. Wengst *Pax Roma and the Peace of Jesus Christ* (London, 1985)

by its activities, cloaks its real goals and identity from those it has taken in. John sees the world's inhabitants falling in line and worshipping the beast. Those who refuse have to live (and die) with the consequences. There are public, social and economic consequences for those who resist: exclusion from regular social intercourse. Without the name of the beast or the number of its name, it becomes impossible to buy or sell.

To summarise:

The Apocalypse offers a change of perspective by its form (visions; disjunctions etc) and content

We need such metaphorical texts to jolt us out of complacency. They may not give us a blueprint for action, for which we will need to turn elsewhere

Apocalyptic imagery beckons us to alternative ways of reflecting on God and God's world. It puts at the very centre the prophetic nature of the church

The critique of empire is more important than accommodation with the principalities of an age which is passing away

It demands that we recognise the inadequacy of the present as we look forward to and work for God's reign on earth as in heaven

Equally, we need to be open to the Spirit, who speaks to the church and the world and enables us to speak apocalyptic words to our generation

If I had the chance now, I would want to go back to my diocese's discussion and ask it to be a community which hears the Apocalypse. I would seek to persuade them that this is not mere rhetoric and what is required are painful choices and costly witness. In the gospel the critical meeting with Christ, surprising as it may seem to all concerned, turns out to be with the needy and impoverished. Ministering to the Son of Man, who comes upon us unawares, is fundamental for any understanding of mission and for any theology. It requires of us appropriate ways of being church and of engaging in theological reflection to match the new situations with which we will be confronted. There is a prophetic vocation which cannot be dodged. This must concern what Blake termed 'minute particulars', which requires of us a specific word, as it did from the prophets of old, not the bland comments to which few will take exception. We shall need to learn new theological skills, such as discernment in particular contexts about what constitutes a faithful prophetic witness to the way of Jesus Christ and to share in the activity of the Spirit who convicts the world of justice and judgement. It is here that the tradition of contextual theology, pioneered in Latin America but found at work in various parts of the First World, is so important. I am glad to note that you are giving space to that in your conference. That requires extraordinary wisdom of spirit which ought to be part of our theological curriculum but is almost completely absent. All this and much more will be required of a church which hears the Apocalypse. It is understandable if the secular initiatives now gathering pace ignore the Apocalypse as they prepare to mark the Millennium. It is important that the church does not, however; and I hope that its perspective may form a part of the vision and your deliberations also in the days ahead.

I
THE MISSION OF THE SPIRIT - THE GOSPEL OF LIFE

Jürgen Moltmann

Let me begin with a number of theses, and then go on to offer a detailed and coherent account of what I mean by the title 'the mission of the Spirit' and 'the gospel of life'.

I. PREMISES

1st thesis: Christianity is in origin and by its very nature a missionary religion.

If Christianity loses its missionary character anywhere in a civilization, or at any time in a given era, or in any society, it is forgetting its origin and surrendering its identity.

The negations of this thesis follow accordingly: Christianity cannot be a family religion, a tribal religion, or the religion of a particular people or nation. It cannot be a male religion. And it cannot be the political religion of a particular government or rule. If these religious forms develop, Christianity becomes so deformed as to be unrecognizable. Consequently Christianity is not dependent on family ties or tribal identity, on a community of fellow nationals, or on male clubs. With its message 'to everyone' it reaches out for the faith of all and every human being, simply as human beings.

This thesis is problematical, as we can see easily enough. Missionaries impelled by a sense of mission and a message are not the pleasantest of companions, because they can make us feel badgered, and won't leave us in peace. The various Christian missionary movements didn't always bring life to the people and peoples to whom they went. Often enough they brought death. Charlemagne's missions to the Germanic peoples, Otto the Great's mission to the Slavs, the Spanish mission to the Indios, the Puritan mission to the Indians, and so forth, presented a *cogite intrare*, where the alternative wasn't belief or disbelief; it was baptism or death. So how can we free ourselves from the burden of the imperial and clerical mission of the last two thousand years, so that we can go forward with an 'evangelisation for the third millennium' which won't be enslaving, but which will liberate, and minister to life? Or should we let missionary efforts go altogether, and confine ourselves to interfaith dialogues?

2nd thesis: Mission is the all-embracing term for the sending of Christ and for the sending of the people who have entered into his discipleship. Evangelization is only one task among others of this all-embracing mission.[1]

In Matt. 11.5, 'the poor have the gospel preached to them' comes at the very end of the list of experiences with Jesus: 'The blind receive their sight, the lame walk, lepers are cleansed, the deaf hear, and the dead are raised up.' According to Matt. 10.7-8, when the disciples are sent out, the exhortation to preach is put at the beginning: 'Preach that the kingdom of heaven is at hand.' That is then followed by 'Heal the sick, raise the dead, cleanse lepers, cast out demons.' The messianic mission of Jesus and the people who are his is one and the same: the coming kingdom which is now approaching - which is 'at hand'- is the substance of the joyful, liberating message which gives fresh heart to the poor, the captives and the oppressed. But evangelisation and the verbal witness to God's coming kingdom and his righteousness and justice cannot stand on their own, in isolation. They belong within the all-embracing charge to heal and liberate the sick and helpless world in the 'at-handness' of God's kingdom. In more recent times people have often put it as follows: Christ's mission is *kerygma - koinonia - diakonia*. In every event, it is a rich abundance of the charismata of the Spirit who was in Jesus and the Spirit whom Jesus gives. The wealth of the life-creating energies of the Holy Spirit is as rich and protean as the whole created world, for these energies are 'the powers of the age to come', as Heb. 6.5 says. So I propose to talk about an 'evangelization for the third millennium' only in this wider context of the holistic mission of the life-giving Spirit.

3rd Thesis: Without interfaith dialogue no one will understand anything. Through interfaith dialogue no one has ever become a Christian.

---

1   For more detail here see J. Moltmann, *The Church in the Power of the Spirit. A Contribution to Messianic Ecclesiology*, trans. Margaret Kohl London, 1977, 2nd ed. 1992, Chap. IV: The Church of the Kingdom of God, 133-196

That means that this dialogue is not a substitute for mission or evangelization. The academic demand that the Chair for Missionary Studies in Tübingen should be renamed Chair for the Study of Dialogue was prompted by complete ignorance both of mission and of religious dialogue. I came across the concept of dialogue first of all in the 1949 Kerkordre of the Dutch Hervormde Kerkof. This says: The church's apostolate consists, first, in dialogue with Israel; second in the work of mission to the nations; and third in 'kerstening'- that is to say, 'the Christianization of one's own people'. I have always clung to these distinctions. We are engaged in dialogue with Israel because we have 'a book and a hope' in common. 'With the gospel of the kingdom of God, we reach out to the peoples in the non-Christian world' (VIII.3). We work so that our own society may be interpenetrated by the righteousness and justice of God's kingdom (VIII.4). So we should avoid any unnecessary generalization of the term or concept of dialogue, because generalization makes it abstract. Today's interfaith dialogue is not the same as the dialogue between Christians and Jews.[2]

We need the dialogue between the different faith communities just as much in Duisburg as in Cairo, in Rome as well as in Mecca. The person who stays put in his own closed circle and stews in his own juice becomes stupefied, because what is no different is for those who are no different a matter of complete indifference. It is only over against other people that we become sure of what we ourselves are.

Through interfaith dialogue no one has ever become a Christian or a Jew or a Muslim or a Buddhist. The dialogue between the religious communities acts as a tranquillizer of the *status quo*. In tendency this dialogue is completely conservative. We all stay just as we are, but enter 'into conversation', so that we can live together. The outcome of these conversations is generally that we are no longer entirely strange to one another, and that we 'leave each other in peace'. Is that supposed to be 'the peace between the world religions' about which my friend Hans Küng is so enthusiastic? No, that is not what he himself wants either.

---

2   On interfaith dialogue, see J. Moltmann, 'Dialogue or Mission? Christianity and the Religions in an Endangered World' in *God for a Secular Society*, trans. Margaret Kohl, (London, 1999.)

But then what is the goal of interfaith dialogue? Unlike the earlier religious disputations held before a king or a city council, in which the subject was 'the true religion and the false' (as Zwingli put it), modern dialogue between the religions has no goal: the way itself is the goal, we are told. In other words, dialogue is the purpose of dialogue. Consequently these dialogues have no outcome other than continued and deepened dialogue. It is understandable that in the countries of the Western world, interest in dialogues of this kind is considerable; for here multifaith societies are supposed to develop, but without disturbing the social peace. But it is also understandable that in Asian and African countries interest in the Western dialogue programme is slight.

Up to now, experiences of dialogue show a number of imbalances:

a) Christians ask; rabbis, mullahs or swamis answer-but they ask nothing on their own account. They aren't interested in Christianity, and know almost nothing about it, their comments being confined to critical remarks about the decadence of the Western world (pornography and so forth). A well-known pioneer of Christian-Jewish dialogue at the German Protestant *Kirchentag* (or lay assembly) said rather sadly to me, after twenty years' experience: 'The Jews never asked me anything.' So we often end up with dialogues between Christians about Buddhism, Islam or Judaism in the face of astonished and silent swamis, mullahs and rabbis. 'Of course you can ask us anything at all', they say. But they ask nothing themselves.

b) Another imbalance is that minorities are interested in dialogue as a way of presenting themselves publicly, but majorities are not. Muslims are extremely interested in dialogue in Christian countries, but deny dialogue to the Christian minorities in their own countries. In Christian countries they demand equal rights, and persecute Christians in the Islamic states.

c) Not least important: the programme for interfaith dialogue is a Western idea, for 'book' religions are of course better equipped for verbal dialogue and logical argumentation than meditative religions such as Buddhism, or ritual religions such as Shintoism. This is already evident from the fact that in the dialogue between the world religions, the 'animist' religions of Africa, Australia and Central America don't put in an appearance at all.

In the *direct* dialogue between the world religions (which used to be called the 'advanced' religions), the nature or animist religions have little to say. But in the *indirect* dialogues which take place at environmental conferences and on Earth Day, they talk about the age-old wisdom of their religions in their dealings with the earth and their fellow creatures. Human life 'vibrates' in the rhythms and cycles of the earth, and 'dwells' in concurrences with the laws of nature. The wisdom of the animist religions in their dealings with the organism of the earth is of course pre-industrial, but it can be translated into the life of a post-industrial society. The ecological catastrophes which affect us all require the 'advanced' religions to 'come down to earth'; and this was in fact the demand of the Parliament of the World Religions held in Chicago in 1994 too. Looking back, we must even ask critically: what destructions of the world have the world religions justified in the past? What resignations hostile to life, and what aggressive apocalyptic tendencies, do these religions harbour - tendencies which must be overcome if the world is to survive? This *indirect dialogue* is changing the religions today, and we must hope that it will change the world too, for the better.

Today *the question of life* has become the question of survival. Here at least four points of intersection have emerged in the struggle against the powers of death:

1. Tens of thousands of nuclear weapons are still lying ready for 'the final solution' of the human race. A nuclear war is improbable at the moment, but the potential for the annihilation of the world can easily get out of hand.

2. It is not just human life that is in deadly peril through more and more 'natural' catastrophes, catastrophes which are actually man-made. The earth's organism is under threat from human domination and depredations, and it can lose its equilibrium and die.

3. Over-population is creating more and more 'surplus people' and victims of violence. When living space diminishes, weaker life is pushed out by the stronger members.

4. In the world of the industrial West - what we sometimes call the First World - apathy towards other life, and towards our own lives too, is on the increase. We are finding it harder and harder to say an unconditional 'Yes' to life. We aren't

investing in the future any more. Instead we are heaping up debts which will be a burden on our children and our children's children.

II. THE MISSION OF THE SPIRIT

In recent years, a theology of life has developed world-wide which gives cause for new ecumenical hopes. On 30 March 1995 Pope John Paul II published the encyclical *Evangelium vitae* in which he set a 'culture of life' over against the modern 'barbarism of death'. Even earlier, in 1990, the 'conciliar process' published in Seoul, Korea, 'the ten basic convictions' for a joint Christian catechism on social ethics. In 1993, in Larnaca, Commission III of the World Council of Churches agreed a study programme on 'the theology of life'. Earlier still, in 1984, Gustavo Guitiérrez book *The God of Life* appeared, as an offshoot of liberation theology (an English translation came out in 1991). The new theological work on pneumatology published at the beginning of the 1990s by myself, M. Welker, G. Muller-Fahrenholz, L. Dabney and others, turns to the Pentecost experience in its search for a new approach to an integral theology of life.[3] Here in actual fact the intentions converge. Whereas the Pope concentrates mainly on the protection of unborn life, liberation theologians focus on the exploited lives of the poor; whereas the pentecostal preachers and theologians see the sick life of the poor, we have before us the apathetic life of people in the industrial West - apathetic because it is meaningless and futile. How would it be if today we were to make the salvation, healing, liberation and affirmation of life the content of Christian mission, and link the mission of life with the gospel of the Spirit who is the life-giver? Let me try.

1. Mission Looking Towards the End

1. Earlier, we knew Christian mission as the spread of the Christian *imperium sacrum*. The salvation of the nations is to be found in their subjugation to *the holy rule* of the Christian emperor, who judges and rules in the name of the God who is

---

3 J. Moltmann, *The Spirit of Life*, trans. Margaret Kohl, (London and Minneapolis , 1992) 'M. Welker, *God the Spirit,* trans J.F. Hoffmeyer, (Minneapolis, 1994); G. Müller-Fahrenholz, *God's Spirit Transforming a World in Crisis*, (WCC, Geneva,1995)- L. Dabney, *Die Kenosis des Geistes. Kontinuität zwischen Schöpfung und Erlösung im Werk des Heiligen Geistes*, (Neukirchen,1997)

both Lord and Father. His rule is nothing less than the Thousand Years' Empire of Christ, or 'the Fifth Monarchy', in which Christ's people will rule the world with him and will judge the nations (Daniel 7, Revelation 20).[4] It was under these auspices that the Christian emperors and Tzars 'missionized' the heathen peoples. The missionizing of Latin America was carried forward in the name of the Spanish king, as the spread of the *cristianidad*. In the 19th century 'Christian civilization', with its cultural mission, took the place of political rule. Today 'the community of Western values' shows only faint traces of the political and cultural messianism of earlier Christianity.

2. We know Christian mission as the spread of the Christian church *urbi et orbi*, from Rome, from Wittenberg, Geneva or Canterbury. The salvation of men and women is to be found in their subjection to the *holy rule of the church*, for its lordship is nothing other than the 'Thousand Years Empire of Christ' in the Spirit, in which Christ's people will rule with him and will judge the nations. The Catholic Church is '*mater et magistra* of the nations', their mother and preceptress. The mission and spread of the churches have also led to the world-wide spread of the divisions among the European churches. Indeed, in the same degree to which in Europe the ancient steeples tottered, and both culture and politics were secularized, through their missions these same steeples became 'secular' in the sense of world-wide.

3 Finally, ever since the 19th century we have known mission as the evangelization of humanity - if possible 'in this generation', as John Mott said. This means awakening

---

4   The theology of the universal Christian monarchy derives from the vision of the monarchies in Daniel 7. The four bestial kingdoms which rise up out of chaos are followed by the kingdom of the Son of man, which comes from God and will remain eternally. It will crush the other kingdoms with 'the stone of Daniel'. The fourth kingdom is the Roman empire, which follows the empires of Babylon, Persia and Greece. It forms a transition to the Christian *imperium sacrum* as the 'fifth monarchy', the messianic empire, which will endure to the end of the world. In the 15th century this political theology passed from Byzantium to Spain and Portugal, and after the discovery of America was used to justify the violent conquest and missionizing of the new continent. I am indebted for this pointer to the 'Iberian quintomonarchism' to M. Delgado, 'Die Metamorphosen des Messianismus in den iberischen Kulturen', *Neue Zeitschrift für Missionswissenschaft*, Schriftenreihe 34, (Immensee, 1994).

personal experiences of faith and personal decisions of faith in other people. Salvation is to be found in *personal acceptance in faith of Christ's holy rule:* 'Accept Christ as your personal Lord and Saviour and you will be saved.' This kind of evangelizing mission is also determined by God's future.

These three forms of Christian mission have one thing in common: they are all determined by *apocalyptic expectation.*[5] The Thousand Years Empire of Christ has already begun and must spread throughout the world before the advent of the last days of terror, Armageddon, Gog and Magog, the end of the world, and the Last Judgement. Fear of the apocalyptic end means that 'time presses', and also presses towards violence. The apocalyptic symbols are evident: George and Michael and their fight with the dragon; the Madonna upon the orb of the world, her foot on the head of the serpent; and the decision of faith which is called 'eschatological'. What they also have in common is that they start from something that is existent now in particularist form, or something that has already begun, in order to universalize or 'globalize' it, whether that 'something' be the *imperium sacrum,* or the church's hierarchy, or the decision of faith. This suggests an aggressive seizure of the whole world, or the rest of it. In 1876, in Leyden, E. Buss published his book on 'Christian Mission, its Justification in Principle, and its Practical Implementation'. He closed with this eloquent passage (p.329):

'We see the earth beneath us lying radiant in a glorious light, the light shed upon it by Christ himself, life's eternal sun. We see a humanity richly blessed, united as brothers in true adoration, in love and peace, rejoicing in the mild splendour of that sun. And we are overwhelmed by the yearning to experience it also, and to help in its coming, that blessed Golden Age of God's kingdom in its fulfilment, the universal rule of Christ's Spirit on earth. So that it may come, we cry here: away from our previous lethargy! and there: away from the one-sidedness of the past! Lift up your heads, O ye gates, and be ye lifted up ye doors of the world, that the King of Glory may come in!'

'The Golden Age' is the Thousand Years Empire of Christ on earth, which will bring peace to the nations and fruitfulness to the

---

5   J. Moltmann, 'Das Ziel der mission', *Evangelische Missionszeitschrift* 22, 1965, 1-14.

earth. Mission and evangelisation prepare the peoples for this age, and pave the way for the coming Christ. True hope doesn't just 'stand and wait'. It helps to bring about the time when the kingdom of God will be fully realized.

But in all three forms of Christian mission the practically efficacious eschatology was *the threat of God's final Judgment*. As the imperial symbols show - the Christian emperor as judge of the nations (in Byzantium and Moscow) and the regimental colours draped in the Christian cathedrals ~ Christian 'mission that looks towards the end' (Walter Freytag) was really always mission that looked towards the Last Judgement. If we are searching for a new approach for Christian mission, and ask about 'the gospel of life', we must first of all, and at long last, Christianize the apocalyptic notion of Judgement, so that instead of awakening fears of hell it rouses hope for righteousness and justice.

Up to now evangelisation has always placed the decision for faith or unbelief in the light of *the Last Judgement*. Then God will pronounce his final verdict: believers will go to heaven, unbelievers to hell. That is still the case even today. The 1992 Catholic Catechism still states (No. 1033) that 'everlasting fire burns' in hell. Modern Anglicans have replaced the fire by 'total non-being'. But they hold on to the idea that 'the reality of hell and indeed of heaven (is) the ultimate reality of human freedom.' Hell 'is the final and irrevocable choosing of that which is opposed to God so completely and so absolutely that the only end is total non-being'[6]. But if the outcome of the Last Judgement consists only in the transcendent places heaven and hell, then there is no earth any more, neither the old one, nor that 'new earth in which righteousness dwells'; so there are no 'earthlings' any longer either - no people of flesh and blood. And there is also no bodily resurrection; etc. etc. This eschatology of the Last Judgement thus proves itself to be an idea that is hostile to creation, Manichean or Marcionite and - to put it bluntly - blasphemous.

In 1992 the American Baptist Church invited me to Washington for a National Evangelism Convocation. Its theme, and then mine as well, was: *'All things new. Invited to God's future.'* On the foundation of this theme I understood that that verdict in the Last

---

6 *The Mystery of Faith. The Story of God's Gift.* A report by the Doctrine Commission of the General Synod of the Church of England, (London, 1995) 198-199.

Judgement about heaven and hell cannot possibly be God's last word. According to Rev. 21.4, *God's last word* is: 'Behold, I make all things new.' If we take that seriously, then the Last Judgement can only be something penultimate. It is only the new creation of all created being for the new heaven and the new earth that is final and eternal. The Last Judgement on world history serves to establish the judging and saving justice of God for all and everything. There can only be new creation on the foundation of God's universal justice (II Peter 3.13). If the new creation of all things determines God's Judgement, then that Judgement is no reason for apocalyptic terror - *dies irae, dies illae*. It is a reason for hope for history: in the end the murderers won't triumph over their victims - indeed they cannot even in the end be murderers. 'Transforming grace' is the worst thing that Hitler and Stalin can experience.[7]

If behind the Last Judgement we see God's new, future world, then Christian eschatology cannot be fixated on 'the end' either - neither on 'the end of the world', nor on 'the end of all things', nor on 'the last things', nor on 'the End-game'. 'Even Christ's end - after all it was his true beginning', said Ernst Bloch once. Eschatology is Christian when it sees in the end of what is wrong, the true beginning. Mission is Christian when, in its gaze towards the end, it looks beyond the horizon to God's new beginning: the beginning of eternal life, the beginning of the eternal kingdom, the beginning of the new earth, the beginning of the glory in which God's 'all in all' will be present. Mission is expectation of the life of the world.

If we take the statement with a pinch of salt, we might say that the imperial and clerical missions were *missions in the name of God, who is both Father and Lord,* and who must therefore be 'loved and feared' above all things as Lactantius said. He is represented on earth by the Christian emperor or the Pope.

Modern evangelisations, in contrast, were *rather missions in the name of Christ,* who in faith becomes our Lord, and brings us together as brothers and sisters in the community of his people.

---

7   J. Moltmann, *The Coming of God. Christian Eschatology*, trans. Margaret Kohl, (London and Minneapolis), 1996, esp. Chap. III.11: The Restoration of All Things, 235-255.

What is now waiting for us at the end of the second millennium and the beginning of the third is *mission in the name of the Holy Spirit*. We can see this from the lightning spread of the pentecostal movement, from the congregationalization of the established church - a church district or parish becomes a congregation - and from the new forms of worship, with their spontaneous enthusiasm: 'Get out of control!' Of course we don't expect the coming of a 'third empire of the Spirit', as did Joachim of Fiore. But what we do expect is that experiences and theological insights into the creative energies of the Holy Spirit lie ahead of us. In their light we shall then understand the fellowship of Christ and the Fatherhood of God in a new way too.

2. The Gospel of Life

In the eternal and original sense, mission is *missio Dei* - God's sending. But what does God send? According to the Biblical understanding (which means both Jewish and Christian) God sends his Holy Spirit before the end of the world as the beginning of his eternal kingdom (Joel 3). The Gospel of John says that through Christ he sends the Spirit *who is the life-giver* into the world so that the world may live. The outpouring of the Spirit on all flesh is nothing less than the goal of Christ's coming, his life, his self-giving and his resurrection. 'If I do not go away, the Counsellor will not come to you; but if I go, I will send him to you' (16.7). Pentecost is not just a coda or an appendix. It is the goal of Christmas, Good Friday and Easter.

The eternal energies of God the Holy Spirit will be poured out on all transitory and mortal life - on 'all flesh' - so as to make it eternally living. That is why in theology the Spirit is rightly called *fons vitae* and *vita vivificans* - the wellspring of life, and the life that makes alive.

But the Gospel of John can also say that what God has brought into the world through Christ is *life;* 'I live and you shall live also.' What is meant is the fulfilled, wholly and entirely living, shared life, *eternal* life. That is how the First Epistle of John (1.1-3) extols this life: 'which we have seen with our eyes, which we have looked upon and touched with our hands, *the word of life-that life has appeared* and we have seen it and testify to you *the life which is eternal.* which was with the Father and appeared to us ... God's creative Spirit doesn't bring this life which has been made eternally alive only after death. It already brings it here and now, before death, through the fellowship of Christ. The Spirit of life whom Christ sends into the world is the *power of the resurrection,* which brings new potentialities for living and a new affirmation of life; for in the experience of this life we experience *God's* indestructible affirmation of life and his marvellous joy over life - the divine pleasure, as people used to put it ('There will be joy in heaven...').

Where Jesus is, there is life, the synoptic Gospels tell us. There sick life is healed, saddened life is given fresh heart, marginalized life is accepted, captive life is freed, and the tormenting spirits of death are driven out. For since his baptism God's Spirit has 'rested' on Jesus and acts through him.

Where the Spirit is, there is life, the Acts of the Apostles and the apostolic letters tell us. For in the Spirit the risen Christ comes to us. The Spirit continues Christ's life-giving ministry, heals sick life and gives renewed health, forgives sins and frees people for a new beginning, and liberates oppressed life from the brute force of the violent. Just as Jesus gathers the poor *(ochlos)* round himself, so Christ's Spirit gathers what is foolish, what is weak, what is nothing in the eyes of the world, so as to put the violent and brutal, the noble and the wise of the world to shame (I Cor. 1.26-29).

The mission of Jesus and the mission of the Spirit are nothing other than movements of life: movements of healing, of liberation, of righteousness and justice. *Jesus didn't bring a new religion into the world. What he brought was new life.*[8] The goal isn't the establishment of any rule, not even a moral or religious one. The goal is 'the new creation of all things', 'the greening of creation'. The eternal life which God's Spirit creates is *not another life* following on this one. It is the power through which this *life here becomes different.* This mortal and temporal life gains a share in the life of God, and in doing so, itself becomes eternal. *'This perishable nature* will put on the imperishable and *this mortal nature* will put on immortality' (1 Cor. 15.53). Eternal life is eternal livingness, as Nietzsche said. We mustn't reduce it to religion and the salvation of the soul. It is new spirituality, and that means new vitality. All God's works - the works of the Holy Spirit too - 'end in bodyliness', said Friedrich Oetinger rightly. So Christian mission isn't concerned about Christianity; its concern is the

---

8   Thus D. Bonhoeffer, following Christoph Blumhardt; see *Letters and Papers from Prison*, ed. E. Bethge, trans. R.H. Fuller, [4th] enlarged edition (London and New York, 1971)

life of men and women. And the church's mission isn't concerned about the church; its concern is the kingdom of God. And evangelization isn't concerned about spreading the doctrine of faith; its concern is the life of the world.

But what is life? Nietzsche, Whitehead and Albert Schweitzer believed that 'life is robbery', because Darwin had impressed on them that the animal sphere is a 'struggle for existence' which is about 'the survival of the fittest.[9] So life is a struggle, and the struggle for life heightens life - though of course only the life of the stronger one. Every life wants to live, in the midst of other life which wants to live too. That wasn't just an objective observation. It also offered the biological justification for the domination of the white man, who thinks he is the crown of creation. Life is robbery: that may reflect the experience of the combative male. Yet life is in origin a gift, as every mother and every child knows. Life is born in pain. It is only for the male 'will to power' that life and death are one. But love distinguishes very clearly between life and death, and gives what furthers life the preference, over against what leads to death. But every time life is robbed, life is the presupposition. One can only kill what is alive. So birth is superior to any death.

Is 'increase of life' the meaning of human life? What is supposed to be increased? Living longer, living more intensively, living more powerfully, living faster? Increase is the term for something quantitatively more. In contrast to that, don't we seek for a new *quality* of living in a 'fulfilled life'? But what is our life supposed to be full-filled with? If, with John's Gospel, we talk about 'the fulness of God' from which we take 'grace upon grace' without end, then that is another word for 'eternal life' and a different category from Nietzsche's 'increased life'. It is the *indwelling* of the divine life in our human life, and the *participation* of our human life in the life that is divine. The creative energies of the Spirit flow within us and make us alive in an unguessed-of way. When we talk about the gospel of life, we mean *zoe*, not *bios*.

What does this mean for a hermeneutic of the biblical writings in the coming 'Spirit who is the giver of life' and for life's history? We shall take our bearings from the following guideline: what is to

---

9   M. Welker, 'Konzepte von "Leben" in Nietzsches Werk', *Marburg Jahrbuch Theologie* IX, (Marburg,1997), 41-52.

be worked out in the texts is *what promotes life*, and whatever is hostile to life will be subjected to criticism:

1. What promotes life is whatever furthers the *integrity of human life* in people and communities.

2. What promotes life is whatever furthers *the integration* of the individual life in the life of the community, and of shared human life in the warp and weft of all living things on earth.

3. What promotes life is whatever spreads *reverence for life* and the *affirmation of life* though love for life.

4. What promotes life is whatever heals *life's broken relationships* and *liberates life that is oppressed.*

5. What promotes life is whatever leads to the *rebirth of life* in hope.

6. What promotes life, finally, is whatever serves *God's covenant with life* and breaks the bond between human beings and death.

7. What promotes life is first and last whatever makes *Christ* present, the Christ who is the *resurrection and the life in person*; for in him and with him the *realm of eternal life* is present and that realm overcomes the destructive forces of death.

8. But life out of life's divine source doesn't just mean full human life. It also means 'deified' life as Paul and Athanasius saw in it the divine sonship and daughterhood of those in whom God's Spirit 'works' (Rom. 8.14). This leaven of the Spirit is not to be found in the Spirit's eternal essence, but in its energies. As I see it, these are not the 'uncreated energies' about which Orthodox tradition speaks; nor are the 'created energies' meant, which were a subject for discussion in Western mediaeval tradition. They are *the creative energies* of the Spirit, which link what is uncreated with what is created, renewing human life from its roots, and making it immortal in eternal fellowship with God.

   In closing, let me turn back to the other religions and religious groups whom we encounter in dialogue. In the context of 'life', the question is not whether other religions can be 'paths to salvation', whether men and women belonging to religions other than Christianity are searching for God and can perhaps find God, and whether, therefore, there can be 'anonymous Christians' among the adherents of other religious groups too, as Karl Rahner surmised - or however we may like to formulate the questions about the theological significance of other religions. In this context, the issue is rather the question about *life* in the other religions, and that of course means the question about life in the non-religious, secular world too. The sending of God means inviting all human beings, religious and non-religious, to life, to the affirmation of life, to the protection of life, to common life and to eternal life. Everything which ministers to life in other religions and cultures is good, and must be absorbed into the coming 'culture of life'. Everything which among us and other people hinders, destroys or sacrifices life is bad, and must be overcome, as 'the barbarism of death'.

In earlier times, the theological location where people discussed the significance for Christianity of the plurality of religions was the doctrine of original sin, and the myth of the Tower of Babel. Today some liberal theologians think that religious truth itself is pluriform, and must therefore necessarily reveal itself in a plurality of religions. For me, the theological location at which people of other religions come into view is pneumatology and, in the doctrine of the Holy Spirit of life, the doctrine about the multifarious possibilities for living, and the rich variety of powers of life - what we call charismata. What forms and ideas in the world of the religions minister to life? Can a religion or a culture become a charisma of God's Spirit for someone, once he or she begins to love life with the unconditioned and unconditional love of God?

According to the earlier classification of the religions under the doctrine of original sin, these people must cut themselves off radically from the 'superstition' of their fathers and the 'idolatry' of their people, if they become Christians.

According to the modern, pluralistic theology of religion, they don't need to become Christians at all, if they have found the divine truth in their own religion.

In my own view, everything a person is, and everything which has put its impress on him culturally and religiously can become his charisma, if he is called, touched and stirred, and if he loves life and works together with other people for the kingdom of God. 'Everyone as the Lord has called them' (I Cor. 7). So there are 'Jewish Christians' and 'Gentile Christians', each of them with their own dignity. There are many different gifts but one Spirit (I Cor. 11.4). There are many forms of life, but it is one life.

II
Mission and Dialogue in a Pluralist Society

Theo Sundermeier

I.

Sociological analyses of our time and society are in vogue. They are clear, convincing, and valid for several years. However, the inner change of society and of economic conditions is so rapid that in the contemporaries' consciousness one new analytic model is followed by another. Just a few years ago Ulrich Beck carried weight by characterizing our society as a "Risikogesellschaft"[1] (risk society). Modernizing has been described as the pressure for rationalisation all over the world, touching on peoples' social and individual biographies. Styles and ways of life change, traditional patterns are modified. The key word "individualisation" indicates that anybody has to create and organize his own world and culture of life. An infinitely excessive demand, including the risk of failure, is asked of everybody and to be performed by everybody. Families no longer live a common pattern, as the composition of "patchwork families" is changing and an adolescent child has to grow up with different fathers and mothers and is missing a continuous frame of life, stabilising his emotions. The consequence of this is that interest is orientated to aims, which can be attained within the short term and that the attempt is made in different groups corresponding to their respective hunger for experience. Another all-embracing term was coined by Gerhard Schulze, *"experimental society"*[2] *(Erlebnisgesellschaft/"societas experimentalis")*: we are looking for the prevailing milieu for self-realization, in entertainment, in progress. The risk of success or failure remains, but it is offset by a network of unity caused by the milieu. This is not a durable network and it does not enable long-lasting relationships. The ties exist for a short term and people are interested in variety. This variety, however, is given by the modern, internationally determined, world-wide economy. Thus,

---

1   U. Beck, *Risikogesellschaft. Auf dem Weg in eine andere Moderne*, Frankfurt 1986.
2   G. Schulze, *Die Erlebnisgesellschaft. Kultursoziologie der Gegenwart*, Frankfurt 1992.

we have become a *"multi-options society" ("Multioptionsgesellschaft")* (Peter Gross)[3], which is another important sociological interpretative term of this age. The understanding offered is not only varied but is aimed at an increase of self-knowledge and of experience, feeling, and pleasure. Briefly, "the multi-options society promises more experience *and* more life"[4]. The consequence is restlessness but also the trivialization of life. There no longer seems to be a comprehensive system of meaning as the hereafter; infinity is in the present world and exists in the apparent infinity of research and attainable aims. The conclusions of the Club of Rome concerning the "limits of growth" seem to be forgotten or are compensated by multi-optional intensity of research and world experience.

II.

Sociological analysis also handles the religions, as these are part of the society and something like the central ferment of culture. In the *"multi-options society"* a comprehensive, all-embracing symbol, connecting the varied network of society, is missing.[5] Without this uniting force, however, society must divide, unless held together by external factors, e.g. by a dictatorship. Sociologically religion is touched on its nerve and challenged in its central social function. Thus, it is no surprise that there are sociologists who are demanding that religions and churches remember, and perform, their central tasks more effectively.[6] Religions have not really lost their importance. A "non-religious age", as Bonhoeffer predicted, has not dawned, although we can see in the countries of the former Eastern bloc, especially in the former GDR, the deforming effects of controlled atheism. However, these experiences indicate how religiosity proliferates if society lacks a comprehensive system of symbols.

How are religions, Christianity included, to react to the challenge of the modern age and, above all, the post-modern age, offering a multi-options society? Primarily two reactions are visible: in a variously shaped world we look for refuge in

---

3   P. Gross, *Die Multioptionsgesellschaft*, Frankfurt 1994.
4   P. Gross, *ibid*, 335.
5   Compare H. P. Siller, *Handlungstheoretischer Gang zu einer theologischen Aussicht auf Kunst*. In: W. Lesch (Ed.), *Theologie und ästhetische Erfahrung. Beiträge zur Begegnung von Religion und Kunst*, Darmstadt 1993, 48–67.
6   Compare the lecture of P. L. Berger, *Weltethos und Protestantismus*, Hanover 1995.

established tradition. In a culture shaped by multi-religiosity and multi-ethnicity, we are looking for an identity group, samples of which we know and symbols of which seem to promise security. For Sikhs and Hindus in England, and Muslims in Germany, it is a matter of course to meet in the temple or the mosque, looking for a home where their language is spoken, their moral and cultural values are preserved and their religious desires are satisfied. They want an unchanged Hinduism, a stable Sikhism, and, as Muslims, they know that, whenever they go into a mosque, they will find the rite of adoration which has not been changed for all the centuries; and that, in the mosque, ethics are taught, foundations of which are unshakeable and, in the Quran, are passed from generation to generation unchanged. A conservative, in some respects a regressive, tendency towards a mild fundamentalism can be the result.

Exactly the reverse of that is the reaction of those who agree to the spirit of the times and in that regain their religious feeling of life. Here a "bricolage"-religiousness[7] arises. They assemble their own religion, as in a supermarket, from the different religions and they pick out everything they immediately require to satisfy their religious and emotional needs. Sometimes it is chanting of Hare-Krishna-people, sometimes Zen-meditation, here a little yoga, if necessary with a tantrical touch to improve sexual ability; a bit of goddess worship is pleasing in a patriarchal society; but also the witch is discovered again as an ideal figure and wise woman; astrology is not missing and there may also be a gram of Christ-religiousness, mixed with the belief in reincarnation, as it is healing and contributes to the ecological balance. Do-it-yourself-religion, patchwork-religion, sometimes – this should be particularly emphasized - with real depth, often only a conglomeration of borrowed symbols: pure religious multi-optionality!

Until now we have only reflected the reaction of the religious "lay people", of the religious "average consumer". However, we also have to ask how the official representatives of the religions react to the radical social changes of post-modernism. The tendency towards a regressive conservatism, which we noticed in

---

7   Compare I. M. Greverus, *Neues Zeitalter oder verkehrte Welt. Anthropologie als Kritik*, Darmstadt 1990; E. Storkey, 'Evangelium und religiöser Pluralismus. Eine Perspektive aus England.' In: *Was glaubst Du denn? Anders glauben, zusammen reden.* Weltmission 96, Hamburg 1996, 6ff.

the followers of the different religions, is also to be found in the leadership circles of the religions, and occasionally the desire for a moderate fundamentalism is expressed, as for example in such Islamic countries as Egypt, Indonesia, Malaysia. This tendency can also be detected in varieties of Hinduism. It can also be observed in Rome, where the return to the conventional, pre-Vatican tradition (Vatican II) is unmistakable, combined with a tightening hold and concentration on the hierarchic head in Rome. Also, in Buddhism, we can notice these tendencies, with the important difference however, that here different means of adaptation are employed. With his missionary offensive in regard to the Western world, which has lost religious orientation, the Dalai Lama is an especially striking example. "Tibetan Lamas are present in the esoteric New-Age-scene and demonstrate an astonishing willingness to adapt to western expectations of being 'missionary'. In centres and monasteries Germans are trained in very intensive three-year-seclusions as Lamas and 'Missionaries' of Tibetan Buddhism. After the collapse of the Soviet Union, the Danish 'Lama', Ole Nydaal, is most easily reached on the Trans-Siberian railway, where he has found a new 'field of mission'."[8] The Dalai Lama practices nothing other than the Buddhist skill of UPAYAKAUSALYA, the "clever use of means", i.e. the adaptation of the Buddhist teaching to the auditors' situation, the clever treatment of different stages of ability to understand. "Solid food of Buddhist teaching and practice for the faithful and the western seekers; an easy going Buddhist ethic of compassion for the inter-religious dialogue; and the milk of tolerance and philanthropy for the general audience."[9]

The *Protestant churches*, how do they handle this problem? How should they answer the challenge?

In my eyes two reactions are unacceptable: the Church may neither go the way of a simple return to behaviour formerly proven worthwhile – thus, she denies her origin as a reforming church, living by the presence of the Spirit who shows new ways in new situations – nor may she go the way of cheap adaptation, by propagating a pluralistic faith, the foremost characteristic of which

8   R. Hummel, 'Anderen Glauben respektieren, den eigenen weitersagen - geht das? Zur Spannung zwischen Missionsauftrag und der Achtung Andersgläubiger.' *In: Was glaubst Du denn?* l.c. 2ff, *ibid* 4.
9   R. Hummel, ibid.

are a lack of ties, a kind of patchwork piety. This way she would lose her identity. Both ways are impracticable even when being presented in a theologically extraordinarily strong way, for example, as in the form of a mild evangelical fundamentalism, which is only oriented to the past and wants to stand on a cemented block of religious belief mistaking it for the "living stone" chosen by God (1 Peter 2,4), the foundation of the church, Christ. Nor may she pursue the way of a pluralist theology of religion, which looks at all the religions through the filter of a nationalistic (or, e.g., Hindu) abstraction and behind all the religions discovers the numinous veil of the *one* divinity, thus losing the concrete immediacy of the Gospel and making it pale into a *mélange* of thoughts with no historical foundation.

The Church will have to find her course between this Scylla and Charybdis. She has to nail her colours to the mast, she has to regain contours and present herself distinctively in picture and message. Today the church looks like a "razed castle", Fulbert Steffenski recently wrote, and he complains that the adherents of "(left) Protestantism" act as if they do not think much of themselves and have an attitude of "grumbling" and "crosspatchyness"[10] towards their tradition and would rather deny themselves than shine. Coming from Heidelberg I would like to extend the comparison. There was a time when the Heidelberg castle was larger than the whole town and absolutely dominated the Neckar valley. Certainly it was good that in earlier wars (at the end of the 17th century) the castle was reduced to human scale and can be seen as fragile and no longer effective as a domineering gesture. But it is just as important that the most beautiful and central part has been reconstructed so that by both destruction and reconstruction the castle has become so attractive that it draws many people from all over the world by its aesthetic splendour.

I think it is a blessing that today the church is becoming smaller, so that once and for all she knows that she should not rule; however, she should also remember her real beauty, so that the truth of the Gospel will become widely apparent and will shine as a light and illuminate the way for many people. In other words: the Church must remember her being and her mission, both being contingent on one another and of mutual influence.

---

10 F. Steffenski, 'Gewißheit im Eigenen und die Wahrnehmung des Fremden.' In: *Was glaubst Du denn?* l.c. 10ff, *ibid.* 11.

III.

In order to define this aim theologically we start at the lowest theological level and inquire as to the being of humanity and of the church at its most basic:

1. Man's nature is, as present anthropologists like to say (Plessner et al), "eccentric", i.e. man stems from beyond himself. He does not get life by his own efforts. His centre is outside of himself. Man does not rest within himself, he cannot create himself and cannot give himself his own character and shape. In other words: man lives and exists on foundations which he cannot lay for himself. In theological language: man is a creation bearing the image of God. However, man has to realize his being as a creature. He does this with his life, his strength, his senses, and his feelings in grieving and in love. He is not autonomous but has to find his foundations and thus become sure of his identity.

    The same is valid for the church: she has an origin beyond herself. She lives on foundations which constitute her, but were not laid down by herself. As man cannot do anything about being fathered or born, so the foundations of the church are with God who has sent his Son and the Spirit as the "Go-between God",[11] mediating between God and man and between man and man. On this *missio dei* the church is based and she has to make every effort to realise this mission and thus to realize her being. The Church is not modelled on heavenly outlines like the Tabernacle and did not come to the earth like the heavenly Jerusalem, but has been built of living stones, as is said in 1Peter (1 Peter 2). The Church is composed of actual, living people, being called to be witnesses. The disciples became witnesses as they were involved from the very beginning, as John says (John 15, 27). The Gospel is not direct mail advertising, which is everywhere the same, and the witness is not a postman punctually putting the direct mail advertising into the letter box. Unfortunately today the church's office bearers often behave in this manner. Being a witness means to testify subjectively and with conviction what you have seen and experienced. When an accident has happened, police need many witnesses, whose evidence may

---

11 J. V. Taylor, *The »Go-between God«.* 1972, fr. *Das Wirken des Geistes in der Welt,* 1977.

vary a lot, even being contradictory. In witness variety is included. This cannot be otherwise, as the witness refers to a matter which happened and has been seen from different points of view. You become a witness to something which has happened. You cannot make yourself a witness. The event makes you a witness. In the biblical terms of witness man's eccentricity finds confirmation and new clarity.

What does this mean with regard to the task of the church? Her being must be accorded to the church. Therefore, Jesus says to his disciples: "You are the light of the world. You are the salt of the earth" (Matthew 5). This is the first and original "Great Commission", more precisely, the central promise of mission, giving the church her being and her ministry. The Church is light. She did not give it to herself, she cannot initiate the light. This is her "eccentricity". She has received it, but now she cannot be separated from light, that is, she is shining or she is denying her own self. There is no third possibility! "The light shines", so Franz Rosenzweig said, "it does not shut itself off within itself; it does not shine to the inside but to the outside. By giving off light, however, it does not abandon itself...! Light gives away ... it becomes visible by totally remaining in itself." [12]

2. Man has not only got his origin from outside of himself, he is and exists only *with* others. Formerly in theology this has been called the "dialogic" or responsive principle of man (M. Buber, Barth et al.). As these terms however are subject to a personalistic narrowness and are immune against the subject-object-scheme, I prefer speaking of the *relationality* of man. The words of a Zulu proverb make the question clear. "Man becomes man through men". No man can be man in isolation. We are people because we are talked to, carried, fed, and loved. It is the variety of relations which goes to make up a life. However, we are not only moulded by relations with other people, but our home and the culture of our narrower surroundings shape our thinking and our emotions. The relationality of man is always very concrete. One does not live universally and in 'the everywhere' but at one definite place and among particular people. That emphasises the variety of ways of life.

---

12 F. Rosenzweig, *Der Stern der Erlösung*, Frankfurt 1988 (first edition 1921), 328.

Multiple relationality also belongs to the nature of the church. As Jesus became a concrete human being and lived at a definite place with definite people, lived and called disciples from definite families, so the Spirit looks for the place where he can settle in order to influence people in their special creational and cultural moulds. Therefore the church is always the church in a respective parish, in a definite locality, with its respective language and culture. The Spirit speaks dialect, one says in Latin America. So, the Church always has to develop contextually, and the Gospel also can only be understood in definite contextual clothing. An eternal, unchanging message does not exist and cannot exist.[13] In addition, there must not be an eternal church, remaining the same at all times and places. This would be a museum but not a residence of the Holy Spirit. Here the plurality of churches and their message finds its basis. We have to accept this and come to appreciate it as opportunity to unfold the various gifts of the Spirit but not look for organizational or structural unity of churches. "The Spirit of God creates a many-sided force field, sensible of differences, in which the joy of creative, enhancing differences is cultivated and in which unjust weakening differences, are tempered with love, mercy and gentleness."[14] Unity of churches can only mean: mutual acceptance and respect for the gifts of the other church.

3. The third dimension of being human is orientation to the future. Man does not rest within himself. He is not a closed system. The eschatological dimension is an essential part of him. The eccentric and relational dimension of being human is yearning for the future. Our life is directed to the future, it is in a state of continual development. This also applies to our religiousness and our faith. This life, Luther said, "is not Piety but becoming pious, not health but becoming healthy, not being but development, not quietness but exercise; we are not yet what we are destined for" (WA 7, 337,31). To know the eschatological dimension means to learn that we do not gain the future but that the future comes to us; and that the most important thing is still to come, the Kingdom of God.

---

13 From mission-theological point of view this is concerning the problem of contextualization. Also see the fine study of Evangelisches Missionswerk: *Schritthalten mit Gott. Das Evangelium und unsere Kultur*, Hamburg 1996; V. Küster, *Theologie im Kontext*, Nettetal 1995.
14 M. Welker, *Gottes Geist. Theologie des Heiligen Geistes*, Neukirchen-Vluyn, 1992, 33.

However, we do not build the Kingdom of God but the Kingdom builds us (Luther, WA 18, 694,26). Therefore the Spirit wants to orientate us to this future and prepare us for it. To this we open ourselves.

Again, the same must be said about church. She is nothing in herself, but looking for the coming Kingdom. In her the forces of the coming kingdom – however broken they may be – will be at work, and dragging people into the coming kingdom, while living and in their dying. 'The Kingdom of God is near' means: from the absolute future it comes into our time, into our sphere and meets our human heart.[15] While church is always bound locally, "the church on the spot", the Kingdom is universal. It wants to draw all people and everything in heaven and on earth into its power and its splendour; therefore the message of the Kingdom is valid for all people whenever and wherever they live. Christ went into the deepest depths of hell, to preach to the deceased even there (1 Peter 3,19); how much more is the church commissioned to go to the most distant horizon of this world, to announce the message of the Kingdom to the living. All people are entitled to come to their true identity in and with this message and to find their ultimate aim in life.

IV.

The triple task of man (as well as of the Church), eccentricity, relationality and the eschatological dimension, his (and the Church's) origin, being and aim, all of these dimensions need to be lived out and realized. It is up to the church to address this and correspond with it in her activities. The Church, brought into existence by the mission of the Son and the Spirit, participates in God's mission in the world. By realizing the three dimensions of her nature, she participates in the *missio dei*. The Church does not have a mission but she *is* a mission, in so far as she *is a light*, shining in the world. It seems that we have forgotten this function of the church and hide her light under a bushel. By that we are denying the nature and essence of the Church. Sometimes people coming from outside the Church can realize her nature more precisely than we ourselves. Christianity, F. Rosenzweig wrote, "must do missionary work. That is as necessary for her as for the eternal people, her self-portrayal in protecting the pure source of blood against strange addition. Indeed, mission work is really her

---

15 Compare A. Peters, l.c. 213.

way of self-preservation.   She is reproducing by extending. Eternity becomes the eternity of the way by gradually making the points of the way focal points."[16]

The triple dimension of man and church results in a triple shape of mission.

1. Our common origin, being God's creatures, the given eccentricity, that of men and of the Church induces the Church to live together with those that are socially and religiously strange to her. The mission of church in this shape means: we are not "the Church *for* others" (D. Bonhoeffer) but church *with* others.   In Latin America one speaks of *"convivencia"* (German: Konvivenz). The Church aims for a symbiosis with those socially and religiously strange to her.   All of us are founded in the creational will of God. This is the basis of the search for the *"symbiosis/convivence"* which is realized in a threefold way: we help each other, making up an 'aid community'; it cannot be otherwise.   Racial or religious differences are not valid.   We give help as well as accept help, however difficult this may be.

2. The second form of realizing this symbiosis/convivence means: we learn from each other. "Convivence" is the sphere, in fact the condition, for the second form of mission which results from the relationality and responsiveness of man and church, dialogue. To the call of the Gospel everybody answers in a different way and fulfils the charism given to him by God.   Everybody responds according to the possibilities of his situation, in his language, culture and social circumstances. This also includes the variety of individual forms of being a Christian, much as the variety of churches.   On its way among the different peoples, the Gospel takes a new shape and conducts the Church into dialogue with other people, religions and cultures. Every dialogue starts by listening.   In dialogue we are becoming learners. This also applies to dialogue with the other religions, since by them also God reigns over the world and speaks to us through them.[17]

---

16 F. Rosenzweig, *Stern der Erlösung*. l.c. 379.
17 The study *Religion, Religiosität und christlicher Glaube*, Gütersloh 1991, 1251, edited by VELKD and the Arnoldshainer Konferenz has persuasively pointed to that.

Concretely, this requires communities to form a community of dialogue in partnership with overseas communities and with local groups of strangers. This also includes changes of perspective, that is, to look at the members of another religion and culture from their perspective, at least for a short time and in the dialogue. More important, however, is the realization that in the meeting there are no "mission *objects*". Where God speaks to man in the Gospel, there man becomes a subject and listens as a subject. The Gospel constitutes him as a subject. Realizing that gives us respect for the other, which is the only basis of a sincere dialogue.[18] We are becoming hearing and learning persons and from that we gain new strength. In such a dialogue we notice that we do not only become better acquainted with the other person but – that is the basic experience of any inter-religious dialogue – also more and more deeply understand our own identity, which we do not have to hide in the dialogue but shall introduce appropriately. Anybody hiding or even – as Peter – denying his own identity in dialogue is unsuited for dialogue. He is as contourless as a razed castle or a burnt out torch and will be no longer interesting for the dialogue partner. No, we shall name the beauty and truth and the reason of our faith and "give account for the hope that is in us". And this we do as people that are willing to listen, to love and to understand the others (1 Peter 3,15).

3. By this also the third form of mission and convivence/symbiosis has been mentioned: the *witness* or as we might call it, "mission in the narrow sense". The witness has two dimensions:

a) The light is shining, it cannot do otherwise. "For out of the abundance of the heart the mouth speaks" as Matthew (12,34) says, and Paul says: "Woe to me if I do not preach the Gospel" (1 Cor. 9,16). To bear witness means to speak from what we have heard and seen, to tell about the great deeds of God.

b) The other dimension of mission in the narrow sense is discernible in the great parable of the royal wedding. The king sends out his servants to invite the beggars from the streets (Matt. 22). Mission is an invitation to accompany

---

18 More details see in: T. Sundermeier, *Den Fremden verstehen. Eine praktische Hermeneutik.* Göttingen 1996, chap. 6.

one another on the way to the meal in the Kingdom of God. Mission is invitation for the feast! That is the reason why 'convivence/symbiosis' may be celebrated already as a festive community. Indeed, the feast is the noblest place of meeting the stranger. The invitation for the common meal is the condition of the possibility to announce the Kingdom (cf. the instructions of Jesus in Luke. 10!). It is the experience of all people engaged in the co-operation with foreigners and in the preparation of multi-cultural co-operation that the feast is the real place to become acquainted with the stranger, as, vice versa, it is the best opportunity for the stranger to perceive us and to get to know us in our identity, as nowhere are you more yourself and, at the same time, with the other than at a feast.

How are we to define the relationship between these three dimensions of the one *missio dei*? They are like the three sides of a prism. If they form a unity, only then will the light be brightly refracted and shine so wonderfully. In another picture: the three dimensions form an isosceles triangle. 'Symbiosis-convivence' provides the base. It is the precondition for dialogue; testimony and structures, respectively, colour the address of the church to those who are religiously and socially strange and constitute her as a community where we help each other, learn from each other, and celebrate together.

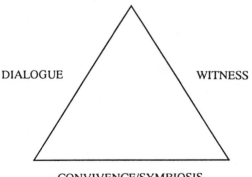

To summarize: the triple dimension of the nature of man, his eccentricity, his relationality and his openness for the future is to be found in the fundamental dimension of the church, which is based upon the *missio dei* and which takes shape as convivence, dialogue and witness/mission. This threefold shape of the mission of the Church, so the study *Religion, Religiosität und christlicher Glaube* (Religion, Religiosity and Christian belief) edited by the Protestant Churches in Germany, says, are not "functions of the church nor her use or value. It is rather the being of the church herself ... the Church happens as mission (sc. witness), dialogue and 'symbiosis/convivence' but not as a proprietary attitude in the possession of her truth for its own sake. Where mission, dialogue and symbiosis/convivence are not vivid happenings, where the care of the *Corpus Christianum* is exclusively in view, there the Church will die. The religions of the world and also the new religious movements should be in the focus of the church's attention".[19] They help the Church to clarify her identity afresh and in the force of the coming kingdom to be what she is, light and salt in the world.

---

19 op. cit. 130

III

Europe - Secularized Or Multi-Religious Continent: How To Speak About God In A Western Society Which Seems To Have Broken Away From God And Religion?

Anton Wessels

I. *Introduction*

In our time there is in the Western-European world a growing alienation from religion and from God. There reigns a kind of analphabetism as far as religious symbols are concerned. Many young people in our societies think that Christ is the brother of Jesus or that Christ is Jesus' surname (*Trouw* 11/11/98). A Belgian author, Kristien Hemmerechts, tells how she drove by car together with her small daughter, Kathy, along a church with a wooden statue at the front when she asked her: 'Mom. Who is hanging there?' (*Trouw* 28/29 11/1998). I learned that in the second largest city of England (Birmingham) Christmas was rebaptized (in something like 'winterfall') and people are in the future going to dream of a 'white winterfall' of whatever the name was (*Trouw* 12/11/98).

A German stage-manager (Jürgen Gosch) coming from the former German Democratic Republic said in an interview: 'The divine what is that? I do not know. I had an atheistic upbringing. Now I try to make up for the damage by reflecting about God. I was born at the end of the war. My father died in it and I was brought up by my mother and grandmother. It was not only a godless youth but also a youth with a lot of women. That shaped me more than that I happened to be brought up in the DDR' (*NRC. Handelsblad* 19 11/ 98).

A Dutch sociologist of religion (Joep de Hart) in the beginning of the nineties made an analysis of hundreds of texts used by young people in which they expressed their image of God. What struck him was the fact that there was a complete lack of any *common* language to speak about God. In any interview with a youngster it seemed a new 'theology' started.[1]

---

1   *Trouw* (Letter en Geest), 4 January 1997.

Yet, in 1998 there was a notice in the newspapers that the play by Samuel Becket *Waiting for Godot* was elected as the most important one in the English language of this (twentieth) century. The British National Theatre had asked more than eighteen hundred playwrights, actors, directors and journalists to select the most popular play of this century. The second place went to Arthur Miller's *Death of a Salesman* (1949), followed by *A Streetcar Named Desire* (1947) by Tennesee Williams. All three from the middle of this century by the way! The Nobel prize winning, Irish author Samuel Becket (d. 1969) wrote the first version of his play in 1952. Is this choice for *Waiting for Godot* an indication that at the end of the twentieth century and at the eve of the new millennium the basic quest for God, waiting for Him, is still with us, despite his declared death by Friedrich Nietzsche at the eve of this century?[2]

In Christian antiquity it was already told by one of the church fathers (Eusebius of Caesarea),[3] that at the moment Jesus had completed his stay among human kind (men) a cry was heard: 'The great Pan is dead?' 'The death of a god or the gods has from of old always fascinated humanity'. 'Hegel tried to understand the death of God and the silencing of hymns and the desecration of holy places philosophically. Not only people but also gods are struck by death. And Moira? (Fate). About her it is said that she stands above the gods. Men as well as gods are subjected to fate. All that lives is mortal; only death is immortal. The withdrawal of God throws man back on him or herself and this leads curiously enough to the return of fate. Man is confronted in a radical way with his finitude.[4] Although modern man is inclined to attribute death to violence, an accident, a medical failure or whatever external factor, man is *essentially* bound to die. With the birth of each human being someone comes into the world who was never before and never will be.[5]

In my contribution I will try to speak about this quest for God in post-modern Europe referring to the possible role of Art, Literature, Music and Poetry. One could speak in this context about the role of the film as well: the cinema as religious or the Film maker as Biblical

---

2   A parallel is in the work of the Egyptian Nobel prize winning (1988) author Naguib
     Mahfuz for instance his story 'Zabalawi'. He describes his quest for God.
3   J.C. Bailly, *Adieu, Essai sur la mort des dieux.* (1993), 101-143.
4   *Drie godinnen. Mnemosyne, Demeter, Moira.* (Boom, Amsterdam 1998) 84, 85, 80.
5   Ijseling, 80.

Theologian.[6] In particular, in my books *Europe: Has it Ever been Really Christian* (London 1994) and *Secularized Europe. Who is Carrying off its Soul?* (Geneva 1996) I have also dealt with the role of film in our modern society. I am prepared to deal with it in the discussion if anyone so wishes, but will not do so now.

It might be seen as something questionable when an appeal is made to art, literature, poetry and music, as we reflect how to translate the Gospel in the world of today. In the past there has always been a strained relationship between the church and these different arts. Even pagan philosophers (like Xenophon and Heraclitus), spoke about the language of poetry as *false*. So one should be aware of what one is doing. In European thinking 'beauty' is often glorified as the *summum bonum* but can also be despised as fraudulent and depraved, seduction and delusion.[7] Thus one should not deny the possible dangers involved. Yet the famous theologian Maria Dominique Chenu called it the greatest tragedy of the last three centuries for church and theology: 'the separation of the theologian from the poet, the dancer, the musician, the painter, the dramatist, the actor, the filmmaker.'[8]

When the collection of Modern Art in the Vatican Museum (Collezione d'Arte Religiosa Moderna) was installed in 1973 and opened by Pope Paul VI he said at that occasion: this collection is the most direct proof of 'art's prodigious capacity for expressing, besides the human, the religious, the divine, the Christian'. On that same occasion the Pope recalled 'the long tradition of friendship between artists and the Church, from which has arisen the artistic and spiritual patrimony, that is mankind's universal heritage'. The meeting place itself was the most moving evidence of this statement. Over the years this collaboration, said the Pope, seemed to have been interrupted: 'the themes of religious art have become tired repetitions of the past, and rules had been imposed on artists that did not leave room for free inventiveness. A clarification had become necessary'. 'We must again become allies. We must ask of you the possibilities which the Lord has given you and the finality which form a fraternal link between art and worship of God, we must leave

---

6   As Ronalds Holloway does in his: *Beyond the Image. Approaches to the Religious Dimension in the Cinema.* (Geneva, 1977).
7   Ijseling, 16.
8   Quoted by Matthew Fox, *Original Blessing.* (Santa Fé), 180.

to your voices the free and powerful chant of which you are capable'.[9]

As explained in antiquity the Muses - who stand for the arts - were born because the gods had the insight that 'man' without art stood dumbfounded *vis à vis* creation.[10] In the Christian era 'the appeal to the Muses was replaced by the invocation of the Holy Spirit'. As soon as praise ceases, the glorification of the gods is in danger.[11] Is God not enthroned on the praises of his people? (cf. Psalm 22:4).

As in the past we cannot, nor should, deny ourselves today these important instruments and tools for the understanding and communication of the mystery of the faith. There are many other media for the message than only the word. 'In the course of the years, one of our modern Dutch writers declared, 'I became more and more aware of a connection, a striking affinity between art and religion and became more and more convinced of the religious character of art - of all art - and the artistic character of ... each religion'. 'Art is a refined human action (...) which evokes emotion'. He calls art and religion 'twin sisters'.[12]

Example from visual art: Vincent van Gogh

In this vein I would like to begin with the art of painting. Since I was referring to the continuing popularity of the play *Waiting for Godot* at the end of this twentieth century, I would like, in the context of our subject, to dwell with you for a moment upon the important figure at the end of the last century: the painter Vincent van Gogh.

Not everyone is familiar with the fact that before van Gogh became the famous painter - of course only after his death! - he was an evangelist in the South of Belgium (Borinage) but also here in the neighbourhood of London (Ramsgate, Ilesworth). It is often

---

9   Mario Ferraza's contribution in: *The Vatican Collections. The Papacy and Art.* (The Metropolitan Museum of Art, New York Harry N. Abrams, Inc. Publishers) New York 1982, 2452.

10 From a column by Marjoleine de Vos, Eeuwige troost (*N.R.C. Handelsblad.* 15/3/99) reviewing Samuel Ijselings book, see note 4.

11 Ijseling, 10, 12.

12 He adds: Art as well as religions know as 'deepest, and essential and never absent theme' of death. In his 'Verwey' lecture De vrouw van Rome in the 'Pieterskerk' in the city of Leyden, cf. Ton Anbeek, *Het donkere hart. Romantische obsessies in de moderne Nederlandstalige literatuur.* (Amsterdam, University Press Amsterdam 1996) 127.

argued that in the year 1880, when he started to develop as a painter he abandoned his Christian faith. It is supposed and argued, even in dissertations, that after this art was replacing religion for him, literature came instead of the Bible, Father Millet the painter and Father Michelet the writer instead of his own father, the church minister. Nature was supposed to have taken the place of God, the sun instead of Christ. I could argue - and have done so about ten years ago in a book[13] - that this is a completely false dilemma and a misinterpretation of both his life and work. For Vincent van Gogh was convinced that art and religion are inextricably linked.[14]

We know Vincent van Gogh both through his paintings and the many letters he wrote during his life. In the context of our subject 'the search of God in the modern age' it is helpful both to listen to him as well as to look at his work carefully. He writes: 'God perhaps really begins when we say the word with which Multatuli (a famous Dutch anti-colonial writer and contemporary of van Gogh) finishes his 'Prayer of an Unbeliever': O God, there is no God! For me (i.e. Vincent), that God of the clergymen is dead as a doornail. But am I atheist for all that? The clergymen consider me so - so be it but I love, and how could I feel love if I did not live and others did not live; and then if we live, there is something mysterious in that. Now call it God or human nature, or whatever you like, but there is something which I cannot define systematically, though it is very real, and see that as God, or as good as God' (Letter 164 December 1881).

'You must not be astonished' he wrote to his brother Theo, 'when even at the risk of your taking me for a fanatic, I tell you that in order to love, I think it absolutely necessary to believe in God (that does not mean that you should believe all the sermons of the clergymen) ... far from it. To me, to believe in God is to feel that there is a God, not dead or stuffed, but alive, urging us toward *aimer encore* (steadfast love) with irresistible force'.[15]

Vincent explained his view that all that is sublime beauty in men and their world - comes from God, and that which is bad and wrong in men and in their works is not of God, and God does not

---

13 *'Een soort van Bijbel'. Vincent van Gogh als evangelist.* Baarn 1990.
14 Kathleen Powers Erickson, *At Eternity's Gate; the Spiritual Vision of Vincent van Gogh* (Grand Rapids, 1998), 3.
15 Letter 161, 23 November 1881. Erickson, 62.

approve of it. 'But I always think that the best way to know God is to love many things. Love a friend, a wife, something - whatever you like - you will be on the way to knowing more about Him'.[16]

He did not categorically reject religion, or even Christianity; he rejected the hypocrisy he had experienced at the hands of the clergy. Vincent painted more than thirty sowers. Obviously he was deeply affected by the biblical symbolism of sowing and reaping - as well as the overtly religious subjects of the raising of Lazarus, the Good Samaritan; and the Pieta, in which he depicted the face of Christ with the features of his own face, 'cannot be understood in terms of an absolute rejection of religion or Christianity'.[17]

Rather than choosing the subject matter and the iconography of traditional religious painting to express the divine presence, van Gogh instead tried to capture what he saw of the infinite in the commonplace subjects of everyday life: 'I prefer painting people's eyes to cathedrals, for there is something in the eyes that is not in the cathedral, however solemn and imposing the latter may be - a human soul, be that of a poor beggar or old street walker, is more interesting to me' (Letter 441, 19 December 1885). Van Gogh imbued the simple figures of sowers, diggers, peasant's children, and even prostitutes with a sacred quality.[18]

Even in his deepest moments of sorrow and pain, van Gogh clung to a faith in God and eternity, which he tried to express in his work: 'there is something noble, something great, which cannot be destined for the worms.... This is far from all theology, simply the fact that the poorest little woodcutter or peasant on the hearth or miner can have moments of emotion and inspiration that give him a feeling of an eternal home, and of being close to it' (letter 248, 26, 26 September 1882).

Vincent told his brother Theo about his passion for books, Michelet, Shakespeare, Victor Hugo, and Harriet Beecher Stowe. For Vincent van Gogh literature did not take the place of the Bible, but he saw it as the means to explain it: 'Now take Michelet and Beecher Stowe, they don't tell you the Gospel is no longer of any value, but they show how it may be applied in our time, in this our

---

16 Erickson, 66, 67.
17 Erickson, 69 and Letter 265, 8 febr. 1883 Erickson, 33.
18 Erickson, 74.

life, by you and me for instance. Michelet even expresses completely and aloud things which the Gospel whispers only a germ of.'[19]

His famous painting 'Still Life with Open Bible' is a good illustration. You see in this painting, next to the large Bible which belonged to his father, who passed away shortly before (look at the extinguished candle!), in front the yellow copy of the book of Zola: *La Joie de Vivre*. Here he is not writing off the Bible, to replace it with literature. The Bible lies open at the text from Isaiah LIII: the Song of the Suffering Servant. In contemporary novels with antiheroes such as Zola's Pauline in *La joie de Vivre,* 'Vincent saw both the Servant in Isaiah and Pauline Quenu as incarnations of renunciation, sacrifice, and charity. But it was fitting that Zola expressed the Servant mission for a new age in the form of a new body, a joyful young girl, and projected its hope into the future in the form of the child she vowed to raise in the midst of darkness and death.[20]

In Victor Hugo's Jean Valjean in *Les Misérables*, he found embodied his notions of Christ who suffers and sacrifices himself in the service of others. He depicted Christ as a glowing light or a blazing sun. The colour yellow itself often implied a divine presence. The yellow encircling Lazarus' head is reminiscent of the halo surrounding the head of Christ in Delacroix's *Christ Asleep During the Tempest*, which van Gogh had previously cited as an artistic source for his painting of the Sower (1888) without the figure of Christ. As such it is an affirmation of van Gogh's experience of the divine in the natural world. The context in which the golden sun appears, radiating over a sower within a wheatfield, is a reference to the teaching of Christ and his admonition to prepare the way to the kingdom of God.[21] The yellow light is symbolic of the divine presence, as well as the resurrection, in van Gogh's *Pieta*. The colour yellow, which van Gogh often used to represent love, particularly the sacred love of God, is here suggestive of the *rayon d'en haut* (light from above). Van Gogh said that he was painting a rising yellow sun, often symbolic of

19 Erickson, 93.
20 Cliff Edwards, *Van Gogh and God; A Creative Spiritual Quest.* (Loyola University Press, Chicago, 1989), 50.
21 Erickson, 100.

rebirth and renewal, and here symbolic of healing as well as resurrection.[22]

The painting 'Starry Nights' is seen as a synthesis of van Gogh's ideas about religion and modernity.[23] In the face of his own often unspeakable suffering, he still hoped that his pilgrimage toward God would bring him, ultimately, peace in an afterlife. Van Gogh's paintings *The Raising of Lazarus* (1890) and the *Pieta* (1889) both deal with themes of suffering and deliverance, while *Starry Night* (1889), sums up his religious journey in a triumphant vision of the mystical union with God.[24] Some of his last paintings reflect 'the sober reality that van Gogh had begun to believe that he was nearing the end of his earthly life and was looking to the hope of eternal release in death'. Van Gogh's *Starry night* mediates between the two worlds of heaven and earth, life and death, the world 'at eternity's gate'.[25]

Rather than the pantheist some historians have imagined, Van Gogh was more of a panentheist, someone who has profound experience of the divine through the natural world, but still views God as separate from nature.[26]

Paul Tillich said about Vincent van Gogh's painting, *Starry Night,* that it was more religious than many portrayals of Jesus in the mediocre art of our time.[27] Vincent said himself about this painting: 'That does not keep me from having a terrible need of - shall I say the word - religion. Then I go out at night to paint the stars'.[28] From his luminous starry skies that reach out for the infinite to the smallest sunflower, the traditional symbol of

---

22 Erickson, 155. Sunflowers were often used as symbols of faith and love. The sunflower with increasing regularity in the landscape of Van Gogh's St. Remy period as symbols of devotional piety and love of God. Here the cypress, which van Gogh had formely described as 'funereal' in a darker sense, represents the longing for the soul of embrace God through death (Letter 541, 27 September 1888).

23 Erickson, 165. (BB 23 June 1888 Van Goghs invocation of the metaphor of the butterfly ... is clear allusion to the afterlife, since the butterfly, because of its metamorphosis from the caterpillar, has conventionally been a symbol of resurrection in the western religious artistic tradition (169). The cypress, the obelisk of death, is the newly formed crescent moon, which recalls Van Gogh's prevailing concern with re-newal and rebirth, the consolation of the end of the spiritual journey - a parallel to Bunyan's light of the celestial City, as it beckons the pilgrim to his eternal home.

24 Erickson, 79.

25 Erickson, 176.

26 Erickson, 76.

27 Erickson, XV.

28 L. 543, September 1888

devotion to God, van Gogh's art reflects his inner search for meaningful faith.[29]

The example of the art of Marc Chagall

Staying with the art of painting but moving to our own time I would like to mention the striking example in our own twentieth century: the life and art of the Jewish Russian artist Marc Chagall. It sounds perhaps strange to quote a Jewish artist here, but is it really so strange?

It is said about the Vatican museum for modern art I referred to earlier that it is not only a catholic museum but contains works by Jewish artists, the most prominent being the American artist, Ben Shahn, with images and texts from the Old Testament. This collection deals with religion, not with catholicism, that is the beauty of it. That is the result of the Second Vatican Council (Mario Ferraza states).[30]

For instance viewing Chagall's glass windows in the church of St. Stephen's in the German city of Mainz one can experience a step by step introduction into the mystery of the Christian faith: while following, as it were, in the spirit, the ever bluer glass to the deep blue ones in the centre above the altar, one gets more deeply initiated into the mystery.[31]

In the preface of the catalogue of the *Musée National Message Biblique* Marc Chagall writes: 'I found it (i.e. the Bible) always and also now still the greatest source of poetry of all times. Always I searched for its reflection in life and nature. The Bible is as it were the echo of nature and I have tried to transmit this secret'.

'I would leave those (paintings) in this house (museum in Nice) to let people find peace, reflection, religiosity and the sense of life. According to me these paintings are not the dream of one particular people, but the dream of all people'. Speaking about colour, Chagall explains that colour transcends all art expression. 'Are painting and colour not carried by love ('love that moves the sun and other stars' as the final words of the Dante's *Divina Commedia* states)? 'Is painting not exclusively the reflection of

---

29 Erickson, 6.
30 *Trouw*, 10/8/1998.
31 Cf. Antonie Wessels, *Secularized Europe. Who Will Carry Off Its Soul?* Geneva 1996, 32, 33.

our inner being?' Colour with her lines is a reflection of your character and your message.

'Because each life inevitably ends, we have to portray (or depict) our life as long as it lasts in colours of our love and our hope. This love is the significance of the logic of any society and the essence of each religion. And for me the perfection in art and life is only to be found in the source of the Bible. Without the spirit of love art cannot bear fruit in life.'

Chagall hopes that both young and old people will visit this museum to find here the ideal of brotherliness and love, 'as I have dreamt it in my colours and my lines'.

'Perhaps here also the words of love which I feel for all will be expressed. Perhaps here there will be no enemies any more and young and old people will build the world of love with new colours, as a mother brings forth a child in love and pain. Far away from all anger and excitement all will come here to whatever religion they belong, - one could speak not only of artistic but also a religious *oikumene* - (will come here) and speak about this dream. And I would like that on this spot pieces of art and expressions of exalted spirituality of all peoples will be exposed, so that one will be able to listen to their music and their poetry which the heart inspires. Will this dream become reality? In art and in life everything is possible when love lays at its basis'.[32]

Literature

As another area of my concern I turn now to literature, although we heard Vincent van Gogh already saying something about it. Again the issue is: how can literature helps us to find answers to the question of the quest for God in our time?

Literature was important right from the beginning of Church history. There was this interaction between the Bible and 'Literature' although this relationship was not without tensions.

The church-father Jerome (d.420) can be quoted as an example of how the church wrestled with the question of how to relate Gospel to culture. He became, of course, known first of all as the translator of the Bible in Latin, the Vulgate. He was a pupil of a famous Roman grammarian (Donatus), who was the author of an

---

32 Pierre Provoyeur, Marc Chagall. *De Bijbelse boodschap*. (H.J/.W. Becht, Amsterdam , 1984), 19, 10.

extensive commentary on literature, especially Terence and Vergil. Jerome in his turn became the interpreter of the Bible. According to him it was possible to build a bridge between profane erudition and the Gospel. Not everything should be rejected and elements of the Graeco-Roman culture can be used and be taken in the service of the spread and the deepening of the Christian faith. 'Did not,' Jerome asked, 'St. Paul also make use of classical authors' (he had several direct quotations from profane literature)? In order to explain the way in which he dealt with classical literature he took the image of the bees, which take honey from some and pass by others: when the Jews left Egypt, they robbed gold and silver from the Egyptians and melted it to use for vessels for the purpose of worship.

Yet Jerome does contrast the *eloquentia* (eloquence of pagan literature) and *veritas* (the truth of the Christian faith). 'We are pupils of the *piscatores* (fishermen) not of the *oratores*'![33] But Christians who had had some education - like St. Augustine and Jerome himself - were to a certain extent bored by the fisher language (*sermo piscatorius*) of the Bible.[34]

But 'literature' also remains in my opinion of crucial importance in our own time. 'A book must be as an axe which breaks the ice of the soul', Franz Kafka said.[35] Being related to modern literature means to be in solidarity with modern man. Modern literature describes the human condition (*condition humaine*). 'Modern man looks in such books for what he found in the past in the dimly lighted, upwards directed vaults of the churches. *He does not kneel any more*, he reads the riddle of his unasked for existence', said a well-known Dutch theologian, K.H. Miskotte, in an interview 1968.[36]

Lately in modern Dutch literature the themes of God and the meaning of life are spoken of again. In 1997 the theme of 'the week of the Book' was 'My God'.

---

33 G. Bartelink, 'Evangelie en profane literatuur in de brieven van Hiëronymus', in: H.S. Benjamins and others, *Evangelie en beschaving; Studies bij het afscheid van Hans Roldanus.* (Boekencentrum) Zoetermeer 1995, 95 , 97, 100, 101, 102, 104, 105, 106.

34 Danny Praet, *De God der Goden; De christianisering van het romeinse Rijk.* (Kok Agora Kaperllen, Kampen 1995, 111.

35 D. Sölle, *Opwellingen van moed. Aanzet tot een andere manier van denken,* (Ten Have, Baarn) 138.

36 Erik Borgman, *Alexamenos aanbidt zijn God. Theologische essays voor sceptische lezers* (De Horstink, Zoetermeer, 1994) 117.

A modern Dutch author (Oek de Jong) deals in one of his essays with the question: 'What is mysticism?' In one of his short stories (*De inktvis*) he tells about mystical experience. In his stories he descends into the interior of his inner world. 'When you deal with the essentials you come across old images', he states (*De Volkskrant* 14/2/97)). In one of his recent books (*Een man die in de toekomst springt*) he explains why becoming conscious of his experience of God was necessary for him as a writer and why his quest took so long. In literature and art he was looking for congenial spirits and hoped to gain useful insights from the sources of Christian and eastern mysticism.[37]

He tells about the effort, together with another Dutch literary friend (Frans van Kellendonk), to arrive at a new image of the world and of God (*De Volkskrant*, 14/2/97). He belongs to that circle of writers who said of themselves that they had 'their heart in their head'. In this century he wrote: 'Enlightenment (*Aufklärung*) went bankrupt ten times over. It is an illusion to think that human nature is good. One can not escape evil and death'. In his reflection about the situation he uses words and images of the Christian tradition. His other Dutch writer-colleagues were surprised that he believed in God and heaven and what lies under the dust of the metaphysical junk-attic. In 1988 he pleaded for the use of the great words of the Christian tradition again, in order to unravel one's own existence. One might abolish the great words, but you cannot abolish the longing from which they have roots.[38]

Modern literature can also have, in our secular societies, a critical function which is in my opinion not unconnected with the prophetic function of the Bible and the Gospel. I would like to mention a Dutch female author (Renata Dorrestein). In her books she copes with the negative sides of our modern culture and society and even tries to exorcize evils. She mentions evil by name: the idea that men claim to be able to forge, shape and form one's own life: think for instance about the whole development of medical science.[39] She wrestles in her books with the suicidal death of her sister. How to cope with the death and loss of a loved

---

37 Cf. Willem Jan Otten, *De fuik van Pascal* (L.P. Boon lezing, 1997), 30. I fell into the trap of their faith (Pascal, Dostoevsky): 'I began to believe that I had to believe'.

38 Borgman in: *De Bazuin*, 1 May 1998.

39 Cf. *Dit is mijn lichaam* [This is my Body]. 1997

one or the devastating effects of incest?[40] How to deal with one's own serious illness? In her last book she tells about a family nearly going under because of the post-natal depression of the mother.

She shows how behind the facades of human life dramas unfold which are mostly invisible to outsiders. She shows however orderly life may look, it is in reality full of chaos, misunderstanding, misuse of power, and destruction.[41]

A beautiful example of literature I found is J.D. Salinger's book *The Catcher in the Rye*. You remember that young boy (today we would think of him as a drug addict) who is searching for his own identity, roaming around in New York finally only welcomed by his younger sister - is it coincidence that she is called Phoebe, one of the names of Apollo? – to whom he finally explains what he wants to do with his life, if he were able to. One of the Dutch translations of this book 'catches' I think the gist of the argument of the book in the title: the 'rescuer', or the 'saviour', of children of New York".[42] Referring to a song 'Catcher in the Rye' the main character tells his sister Phoebe that he imagines himself to be in the rye while a number of children are playing in it near to a large and very dangerous abyss. Any time they are about to fall into that abyss, he wants to catch them, to save them. The moving thing about this book is that he who himself, in his miserable condition as a young boy, and not knowing where to go, someone who has lost all hold on life (Holden is his name!), is drawn into the abyss himself but wants (when he is asked what he want to do with his life) to become a saviour for others!

A wounded healer, a striking modern parable which touches what the Gospel is all about. The secret of Jesus' ministry. The wounded healer.

Music.

I turn now to music. One can speak about the presence of God in the *sacraments* when they are consecrated. In the tradition of the sixteenth century Reformation the consecration finds place as it

---

40 *Verborgen gebreken.* Uit. Contact. 1996.
41 Dirk Zwart *Horizon* 21 June 1996.
42 *De kinderredder van New York. The Catcher in the Rye.* Vertaald door Max Schuchart. (A.W. Bruna en zoon), Utrecht, Antwerp, 1947).

were in the *sermon*, the preaching of the Gospel. But is it also possible that this consecration takes place in *music and song?*

Music is something very mysterious to me and to many of us. 'Every musical performance, every staging of a play, is an act of pure hermeneutics, an explicative figuration of meanings', George Steiner says.[43] Philosophic anthropology has it that music preceded speech. Schopenhauer affirms that if our universe was to cease, music would endure.[44] Certain theologies or metaphsyical paradigms seek to conceptualise God as 'thought thinking itself', as the absolute willing itself into being and creation. Leibnitz took music to be God's algebra. 'All I know', George Steiner states is 'that music is a *sine qua non* in my existence. It reinsured what I sense to be or, rather, search for in the transcendental. This is to say that it demonstrated to me the reality of a presence, of a factual 'thereness', which defies either analytic or empirical circumscription'.[45]

There has been in the church some apprehension over the sensuality of lady Musica.[46] Yet already in the Old Testament the revelation of God is connected with music. 'On the morning of the third day there were thunders and lightnings, and a thick cloud upon the mountain, *and a very loud trumpet blast,* so that all people who were in the camp trembled' (Exodus 19:16). The wall of Jerico fell liturgically. The prophet Elisha received prophetic inspiration with the help of music. The evil spirit of Saul was exorcized by David's music which brought him temporary relief (1 Samuel 16:23). In the New Testament we hear about the song of Mary, Simeon and Zacharias and the singing of psalms and hymns (Eph. 5:19, Col 3:16).

The old church was in the beginning sober as far as the use of music was concerned. For music might weaken the will and engage people in licentiousness. But, very early on, spiritual songs were used and the Christian church became a singing community. Ambrose of Milan introduced hymns.[47] St. Augustine defended its

43 George Steiner, *Errata. An Examined Life.* (Weidenfeld and Steiner), 22.
44 Steiner, 65, 67.
45 Steiner, 75.
46 *Trouw* 10/10/98
47 Jan Koen, *Voorbij de woorden. Eassys over rock, cultuur en religie.* (Averbode, Ten Have, Baarn 1996) 195.

use. The liturgical year is seen as one of the genial discoveries of Western culture.[48]

Nine centuries ago Hildegard von Bingen composed sacred music and wrote litugical songs. In the *Song of Songs* she found a great source of inspiration. According to her, music was a gift of divine origin. For all that lives and breathes is called upon to praise God. Psalms and hymns make us receptive of divine presence. Music without words found favour in her eyes. *Very striking is her following observation. She saw a connection between 'word' and the humanity of Jesus, while music was kin to the spiritual and harmonic unity of the divine Trinity.* This was a striking idea: to see the word as the particularity of the human situation, and music as a reference to the higher, trinitarian reality wherein the human and the divine flow together in a harmonious humanity.[49] This might give us a sense of the search for God beyond words.

In Mission and Evangelism the importance of music was always felt. The Salvation Army is a case in point. Was it William Booth who said why should only the devil have good music? The Moody and Sankey favourites, songs of the time, could be understood by a child and would not be forgotten. (What a friend we have in Jesus). These melodies were catchy and became hits in the streets. How popular they were became clear one day in a circus in London, when a clown mocked at those Moody and Sankey favourites. The audience started to sing these songs until the clown had to leave the ring.[50]

In the secular word of today it is of importance not to forget to mention pop-music. In a lot of texts of popular music (pop music) there is nearly a kind of mystical longing for freedom, fullness, even the search for eternal life. In one of the songs of the group *Oasis*: You and I are gonna live forever

> 'Live forever'
> Maybe, I don't really want to know
> because I just want to fly
> lately did you ever feel the pain

---

48 F.W. Gorsheid, G.P. van Itterzon, *Christelijke Encyclopedie*. Second Impression Kampen, (Kampen 1956-1961), *sub voce.*, Muziek.
49 Koen, 198.
50 J.C. Hoekendijk, *De kerk binnenste buiten*. (keuze uit zijn werk) (Amsterdam, 1964), 114, 115.

in the morning rain
as it soaks you to the bone
Maybe I just want to fly
wanna live
don't wanna die
Maybe I just wanna breathe
Maybe I just don't believe
Maybe you're the same as me
we see things they'll never see
you and I are gonna live forever
Maybe I will wanna be
now is not the time to cry
now's not the time to find out why
I think you're the same as me
we see things they'll never see
you and I are gonna live forever.[51]

VII. Conclusion

How are we to speak about God in this post-modern situation of
Europe today? At the beginning I stated that there are other media
than only the word. I do not want to suggest that one can do
without words or that one should not try to continue to tell the
Story. Jean-Francois Lyotard has made the extreme case that no
'grand stories' (les Grand Récits) can any longer claim assent.[52] If
so why not - thinking of the Bible - begin with its small stories?
Scriptures are not texts, explains Wilfrid Cantwell Smith. He
means by that saying, that the texts are rather narratives or
scenarios about episodes of life, which ask for performances and
iconography, more than for reading only. Who Jesus is and what
the message about the reign of God really implied, cannot be fixed
in definitions of faith, but only be disclosed in the stories told by
Jesus, like the parables of the kingdom, or by people who have met
the secret of the reign of God in some new and liberating
experiences of a gracious presence of God (C.S. Song).[53] The
Biblical scholar Walter Brueggemann, asks for attention for the
small stories in the Bible. I want to urge 'that our proper subject in
each case is the specific text, without any necessary relation to
other texts or any coherent pattern read out or into the text'. It is
evident that this approach is congenial to post-modern perspective,

51 Jan Koenot, *Voorbij de woorden. Essays over rock, cultuur en religie.* (Averbode,
    Ten Have Baarn, 1996).
52 Walter Brueggemann, *Texts under Negotiation. The Bible and Post Modern
    Imagination.* (Fortress Press (Minneapolis, 1993), 8.
53 Anton Houtepen in: Anton Houtepen ed., *Ecumenism and Hermeneutics* (Utrecht,
    1995), 15.

as it focuses on 'little' stories to the disadvantage of the 'great story'. Focus on the little story requires us to be, to some extent, free of systematic perspective, and especially of systematic theology. The imposition of modern critical or systematic theological categories upon the text has led us to read the text according to Hellenistic modes of rationality that have come to have most credibility in the modern world. Such a synthetic, rational approach, however, has required a violation of what is most characteristically Jewish in the text. For Jewish reading honours texts that are disjointed, 'irrational', contradictory, paradoxical, ironic, and scandalous. In Bible reading new texts require us to re-read everything of God, self, and neighbour in light of neglected texts.[54] Athens and Geneva together have conspired to suppress (texts), and Jerusalem has often been a willing accomplice. That suppression has been in order that the rationalistic hegemony of modernity could prevail, or that the domination of church orthodoxy could control.

The Bible is the *compost pile* that provides material for new life. As it is often with such compost, it contains seeds of its own. Thus I propose, as a way of moving beyond eighteenth-century absolutism and beyond nineteenth-century developmentalism, that biblical faith as drama for our time and place is a way of reading that respects and takes full account of the text.[55] I submit that this way of reading the text (and reading our life) contains enormously helpful access points for pastoral care. The Bible provides a script (not the only script available) for a lived drama that contains all the ingredients for a whole life. The Bible offers many small dramas, some of which are not easily subordinated to the large 'drama of salvation'. As the Bible does not consist in a single, large drama, but in many small, disordered dramas, so our lives are not lived in a single, large unified drama. In fact, we are party to many little dramas. Brueggemann's argument is that the little dramas of the text need to be taken seriously. The little dramas of our lives do not all readily fit into the large, visible drama. As we take up these 'little' texts, it may become clear that my method seeks to avoid the tyranny of criticism as much as the tyranny of authoritarianism. These texts do not need to be explained or justified. They need

---

54 It would be possible to study Karl Barth from the perspective of the neglect of many biblical texts.

55 Brueggemann, 58, 60, 61, 62, 67.

only to be told, as resources for the imagination, left there in that secret zone of intimate reflection to do their own hidden work.[56]

But we have been pleading in this paper for the role of art, literature and music in connection with the quest for God.

Like any expression of culture: art, literature and music can be very ambivalent. It can be used and has often been used in a wrong way. There is a negative side to music as there is to any kind of culture. 'Music can be abused when it is composed and executed in glorification of political tyranny, of commercial *kitsch*. It can be played, indeed as it has been, loud enough to cover the cries of the tortured'.[57] (Cf. Gunter Grass *Blechtrommel* [*The Drum*]). Such abuse can be made in exploitations of Wagner's music and even of Beethoven's Ninth.[58] Music can madden, as it can help the broken mind, as it was in the case of Wittgenstein when he recorded that, more than once, the slow movement in Brahms' Third Quartet pulled him back from the brink of suicide. If music can be 'the food of love', it can also trigger the feasts of hatred.[59] A conductor asked about performing Wagner's opera said: What do you think about certain pieces from *Die Walküre*?: 'You are hearing the entrance of Göring' (28/8/98 *NRC Handelsblad*).

I still belong to the generation who heard the German soldiers singing in our streets. One of my very old neigbours (about ninety now) a teacher of the German language studied in the thirties in München (Germany). He once attended a party meeting in Nürnberg. It was Goebbels who was responsible for the orchestration of those events.

1. The meeting started with the singing of ordinary popular songs like: Der Mai ist gekommen die Baume schlagen aus.

2. Followed by Wanderlieder. Das Wanders ist des Müllers Lust.

3. Then followed Marsliedren.

---

56 Brueggemann, 67, 70, 71.
57 Steiner, 72. Strange example: music was used in a Roman hospice where many people were staying when a mother had to give birth.
58 Steiner, 72.
59 Steiner, 73. But when harnessed to a national or partisan anthem, to the hammer-thrust of a march, the same choral practices, in an identical key, can unleash blind discipline, tribal mania and collective fury (76). Cf. the use of a Dutch Christmas song at football matches of the club Ajax: 'De herdertjes lagen bij nachten'.

4. Fighting songs (Kampflieder): Die Fahne Hoch die reien fest geschlossen.

5. Finally the Führer entered with der Nadenweilermarsch. When Hilter was present the Horst Wessel was sung.

This use of music was known from the time of the emperor in Berlin in 1914, comparable with the SA in Berlin in the Nazi period.

What is true for music also holds for literature. One of the most important Dutch writers - at least so he thinks of himself - (Harry Mulish) when he was asked about the theme of the week in the book 'My God' said that he saw himself as a God being a 'creator' himself. This kind of *hubris* naturally is also found and shows the ambivalence of any art and thus also literature. It can be used in a wrong way. For some authors in the past (like Albert Verwey) poetry announced itself as the substitute for Christian liturgy, as a replacement of religion. A Dutch poet, Jacques Perk, said in a poem (Deinè Theos):

> O beauty, O thou hallowed name
> Thy kingdom come, besides you I worship no other god on earth.

Characteristic for the church father Jerome's life, was the tension he felt. His life became dominated by a dream. He saw himself standing before the throne of Christ where he received the reproach of having been more Ciceronian than Christian: *Ciceronianus es, non Christianus*. He then took an oath never to read any profane authors any more. He stuck to his oath for the rest of his life.[60]

Although one should always remain aware of the possible dangers involved and the abuses which take place, yet I want to plead for the positive use of it. It is not replacement I am looking for of course, but art, poetry and music as interpreters for religion and the search for God. In our secular world poetry might call up sacred experiences.[61]

'All poetry is a profane, worldly (secular) mysticism', said a Dutch poet (Martinus Nijhoff).

Yet I would like still to plead for the possible positive use of arts. My last example is taken from poetry. In an interview, Hans-

---

60 Bartelink, 100.
61 Anbeek, 129.

Georg Gadamer quotes Aristotle who said 'historiography is less directed towards the truth than poetry. Historiography only tells how things *happened*, while poetry tells how things *always can happen*'.[62]   I would finally like to give an example of this, a modern poetical answer to the question I tried to raise in my paper: how to speak about God in a western society?   One of the famous Dutch poets in the middle of this century, Martinus Nijhoff, once wrote a poem at the time when an important bridge was built connecting the two sides of an important river, linking the North and the South of the Netherlands.

The poem is called: 'Mother the woman'.

> I went to Bommel to see the bridge
> I saw the new bridge. Two banks (of the river) which
> seem to have avoided each other before
> became neigbours again. The ten minutes that
> I lay there in the grass, drunk my tea,
> my head full of landscape, far and wide-
>
> I heard a voice sounding over the river
> A woman's voice. The ship she sailed
> came slowly downstream passing through the bridge
> She stood there on deck alone.
> she was standing at the helm
> and what she sang I heard were Psalms
> Oh, I thought, if this were my mother.
> Praise God, she sang, His hand will protect thee.[63]

A contemporary Dutch poet, Rutger Kopland, made a recent poem which is inspired by this example.   Here a poet has the floor who claims not to be religious, an atheist and secular modern man. He speaks in this poem about a visit to his mother in an old people's home.

The poem is called: 'Mother, the water'

> I went to mother, to see her again
> I saw a strange woman. Her look was wide
> and empty, as if she was staring at the far (beyond) otherside
> of the water, not at me. I thought perhaps
> - when I stood at the lawn of the nursing home,
> the time went by slowly in the Godforsaken solitude-
> maybe it would be good if Psalms now sounded
> It was my mother, the small body standing in the grass.

---

62 Quoted by Marjoleine de Vos, Schikgodinnen, *NRC. Handelsblad* 26/4/99.
63 *Verzamelde Gedichten* (Prometheus, Bert Bakker, Amsterdam, 1995) 232

Only her thin hair was moving a little in the wind
as if she was moving on quiet waters to an endless there and
later, her God. There is no God, but I swore to Him that He
would keep His promise, to protect her.[64]

---

64 Rutger Kopland in his newest book *Tot let ons loslaat* (van Oorschot, Amsterdam, 1998), 16

IV

'Reflections on Stavangar' – A European missiological conference (August 1998)

Timothy Yates

I am grateful to the BIAMS executive for this opportunity to make a presentation on the European conference at Stavangar last August – it was unsought but I believe there is a good deal to be gleaned. The background to the meeting was an initiative of Professor Jan Jongeneel of the University of Utrecht – some of you will know his remarkable mission encyclopedia in two volumes *Philosophy, Science and Theology of Mission in the nineteenth and twentieth centuries* of which the second volume appeared in 1997 dedicated, with other mission associations, to BIAMS. At the IAMS (International Association for Mission Studies) meeting in Buenos Aires, he had invited a number of European participants to gather and suggested the need, not for another superstructure to compete with IAMS, but a European network and conference meeting between IAMS conferences every four years: so if IAMS meets, as it will, in 2000 the next in this series would be 2002. The aim would be to address specifically European missiological issues, to construct a directory of mission agencies and teaching institutions and to share concerns. The basic participants would be the European associations to which his book was dedicated – NIME (Nordic Institute for Missionary and Ecumenical Research), who did in fact act as hosts at Stavangar, adding our conference to their own annual gathering, BIAMS, DGM (Deutsche Gesellschaft für Mission) and CREDIC, the French association (Centre de Recherches et d'Échanges sur la Diffusion and L'Inculturation du Christianisme). The conference were greatly indebted to Dr Tormod Engilsviken and the staff of the School of Mission at Stavangar for all the administration of the conference. A Hungarian delegation had also been invited but had to cancel – there is a school of mission in the Reformed tradition in Budapest headed, I think, by a Dutch woman teacher. We were also privileged to have two Russian Orthodox priests, one of whom (Professor Vladimir Fedorov) made a presentation and the other (Fr. Sergei Chirokov) who plans mission study at Selly Oak. In addition, we benefited from the NIME conference just held, where experts like Professor Jesse Mugambi from Nairobi and Professor

Chung, an able female Asian scholar, and Professor Robert Schreiter from Chicago stayed over and gave us the benefit of their wisdom in various interjections. For me the Orthodox presence was particularly notable: and Archpriest Fedorov also preached at the conference service at the Utstein monastery on Sunday.

The missiological issues addressed, of special relevance to Europe, were Islam and New Religious Movements. BIAMS members may need to be reminded of the number of mission departments, with chairs of mission, which exist in European universities so that we had representatives from Uppsala (Professor Hallencreutz, now emeritus) Lund (Professor Aasulv Lande), the Free University of Amsterdam (Professor Antonie Wessels, with us here), Helsinki (Professor Ruokanen), Heidelberg (Prof. Sundermeier), Leiden (Professor Camps) and Utrecht (Professor Jongeneel). In the UK we have the chair in Birmingham (Professor Ustorf) and in Edinburgh (Professor Kerr), who also heads up the Centre for the Study of Christianity in the NonWestern world, bequeathed to us all by Andrew Walls' remarkable pioneering efforts: but although we have a number of universities which either have mission centres (as the Oxford Centre for Mission Studies and the Henry Martyn Centre in Cambridge) or offer courses in mission like Leeds, Sheffield (Cliff College), the University of Wales at Cardiff and various teaching institutes and colleges in Northern Ireland and beyond the UK in Eire, we are still at a disadvantage. In the case of Islam, however, Professor David Kerr was given the opportunity ot treat Islam from a Christian perspective and a female academic from Lund, Dr Roald, to treat it from a Muslim perspective – she herself had converted to Islam after studies in Oslo and she wore the veil, providing a visual image of Islam in Europe. In the light of the events in Bosnia and Kosovo, Professor Kerr admitted that he approached the subject with discomfort and with more of a sense of menace than promise. The basic thrust of his paper expressed his own disillusionment with what he termed 'the liberal Christian conception of dialogue', of which he had himself been, we must say, a distinguished initiator and protagonist. He now preferred the way of *diapraxis*, a term culled from a Danish professor. He drew on his experiences in Hartford, CT, where a drug ridden society, especially among the youth of the two communities, had pressed the Afro-American Christian community and the Afro-American Muslim community to combine to rid the town of the problem. He stressed the need for a *tertium quid*, a focus beyond the respective beliefs and stances of the religious traditions, though he conceded the advantage in this case-study of shared ethnic and cultural backgrounds. It provided a striking and memorable example. Dr Roald was an academic with a feminist background. The main thrust of her paper, which included careful exegesis of the Quran, notably at 4:34 where the man is to take full care of the woman (she made the comparison to Gen 3:16 where *mashal* speaks of control/mastery) to seek to show that the view of women in Islam generally held was a caricature. The teaching of the Quran and the practice of the prophet himself (on record as taking part in domestic work) pointed in her view in a more liberated direction. Those who read their BIAMS newsletter carefully may remember James Anderson's comment: 'those present found it difficult to understand her position, which seemed to be to justify Muslim customs as valid in the modern world, rather than being somehow 'primitive'.' That was a fair summary. It was good however to have a convinced Muslim speaking in such a context.

On the NRM's, Professor Fedorov, who runs an institute one of whose functions is to examine these (he is both vice-rector of the Russian Institute of Humanities in St Petersburg and also Director of the Orthodox Research Centre of Missiology, Ecumenism and NRM's) told us that this was a subject hardly ever out of the papers in Russia. There was great need for analysis of the wide variety of these movements by people who understood religion from within. He used the analogy of poets assessing new poetic forms and musicians new forms of tonality and musical expression. In Russian schools, confessional RE teaching is not possible in the state sector. Directors of Education were open to appointments from the NRM's, seemingly viewed as 'non-obscurantist', while State money was impossible to raise for such missiological institutions as he was running. Religious studies in Russia had become a euphemism for 'scientific atheism'. Understanding of religious realities was unlikely to come from such quarters. Unity, in the form of the 'unification' of the Moonies, and the acceptance of all religions as practiced by the Bahai faith or the so called Krishna-consciousness followers was attractive in Russia as was what he called 'sectarian love' (which I took to be the deep corporate commitment of some cults). Professor Jongeneel's paper attempted both a categorisation of these various movements and an account of the research and resources available to understand them.

In Britain he mentioned the INFORM centre at the London School of Economics and Politics directed by Eileen Barker, the equivalent called CESNUR in Turin and RENNER in Aarhus, directed by Johannes Aagaard, member of IAMS. They all give objective information and careful reflection, without antagonism to the movements. He referred to Eileen Barker's two books, *Of Gods and Men* (1983) and *New Religious Movements* (1995); and, of other books in the 1990's, the cult book by James Redfield *The Celestine Prophecy* of 1993 and Robert Towler's *New Religions and Old Europe* of 1995 with a Penguin *Dictionary of Religion* of 1997. I make one quotation: 'it only surprises that the children and grandchildren of Jews and Christians, who have turned away from ontocracy to theocracy and salvation history, ... return to 'nature' (earth, water, fire, air, ether, etc) and its 'spirits' – please give us that old time natural religion', a judgement which resonates with me and experience of local variations, whether in the Sheffield 9 o'clock service or other contexts.

Before opening up this session to questions and responses, including comments from James Anderson and Antonie Wessels who were fellow participants, I will try to round up some other helpful contributions. Professor Jesse Mugambi, who had made a presentation at the NIME conference before this, responded to Professor Kerr's 'diapraxis' emphasis by saying he preferred to call it 'struggling together for life'. He also called on missiologists to correct stereotypes in the press: for example, to write of the Muslim north against the Christian south in Sudan was a fundamental misrepresentation of what is going on there. David Kerr agreed on both counts and added that Muslims, brought up on the Quran and Hadid culture, were not at ease with the sound-bite world. For Christians, his own Centre for the Study of Christianity in the Non Western World in Edinburgh offered courses on media and religion. Asked by Professor Jan-Martin Berentson if he regarded shared prayer as an essential prelude to social action, he responded that, like the questioner, he had concerns about inter-faith worship but wondered if turning to God in the struggle for justice, akin to Latin American struggles, with the struggle providing its own forms of spirituality, was a different thing from inter-faith worship? In a response to Dr Roald, Professor Chung, as an Asian woman academic, told the lecturer that Asia did not need feminism, as Asians already possessed a philosophy of reciprocity. She saw Dr Roald, a Norwegian who had converted to

Islam, as being in a boundary situation and was herself uneasy with men talking about the role of women. She indicated a clash between the cultural integrity of Islam and the Declaration of Human Rights. Professsor Fedorov reminded us how culture-bound we all become and that this applied to our interpretation of our sacred texts, also: in his view 'veiling' was permitted in Islam where (another difficult issue) female circumcision was not – Dr Roald had insisted that the latter was not an Islamic practice and, if it occurred, it also occurred in Coptic Christianity. To Professor Arnulf Camps, who suggested in criticism that she was taking the debate back to old issues from which he felt Dr Kerr's paper had been a liberation, she replied that she, too, was trying to free things up for the new millennium and that, contrary to many assumptions, Islam was not immutable, any more than Judaism or Christianity. So, she seemed at this point to share common ground with Professor Chung, who had said that change was the important thing.

The term 'fundamentalism' was identified by Professor Wessels as a dangerous one, a term with Christian provenance, inapplicable to Islam and used usually to express bad experiences with extreme Muslims by Westerners. Professor Fedorov was prepared to admit that there were certain forms of Orthodoxy which could be called 'fundamentalist' and who related to NRM's by claiming a sole monopoly on truth for themselves; but others were more open. His own institute had been founded after experience in Hamburg and Aarhus and their missiological departments and chairs of mission and ecumenism. Professor Mugambi asked how open Orthodoxy really was? The so-called 'Army of Salvation', a traditional group, had been legislated against along with the NRM's. He offered the resources of his department in Nairobi by way of e-mailing on the question of the NRM's. Dr Jorgensen indicated how the NRM's again and again pointed up the lacks in the churches and their presentation of the gospel – the view of the cosmos, of nature, of bodies, of spirituality all often defective: general orthodoxy on the gospel was not matched by appreciation of the wider implications of the gospel, as, for example, had been the case in the Celtic tradition – should we reconsider syncretism? Professor Jongeneel agreed that we had not presented a full gospel and had often been too rational. It was suggested that NRM's came in three categories – pre-Christian, Christian and post-Christian. Finally, Dr Ruppel of the WCC staff, high-lighted concerns towards the recent Harare meeting – religious plurality and fragmentation and what often resulted from this in modern life as worrying elements, individualism as against life in community and dehumanisation, leading to loss of respect for human life.

Conclusion

What of the future for these gatherings? Although Professor Kerr offered hospitality in Edinburgh for 2002 Professor Jongeneel is anxious to draw in more Eastern and Southern Europeans and a setting in Southern Europe is more likely. Professor Camps has been made anxious by a new RC confessional network of mission scholars which he fears may imperil the participation of that church's representatives in IAMS: he had intervened strongly against such a move. In general, and for this participant, the involvement of a Romanian lecturer in mission, Fr Petraru, who teaches in Iasi, and the Russian participants already mentioned, held great hope for the future – they had even achieved, to their great delight, the translation of David Bosch's *Transforming Mission* into Russian by a Russian American in Cambridge and appealed for further resources in the Russian language. I must close with renewed appreciation to Professor Jongeneel, indefatigable as scholar and networker and animator for mission studies in Europe; and congratulate him on a vision realised at Stavangar, full of possibilities for the future.

V

Case Study (1)
The Furnival

Revd Jane Grinonneau (Sheffield)

Being open to the dynamic energy of God, leads to endless surprises and adventure! Let me take you to the North-East of Sheffield City, to the City's Number One area of poverty - and tell you a story of what God is doing.

The Churches had pulled out from this area, with one notable exception, that being the Methodist Chapel in Lopham Street, located in the heart of this bruised estate. Notable, not for its size or capacity, there were only four people and their combined ages were a little under 300 years; surely not for its financial resources having, as it did, an income of about £30 a month. What this faith community *was* notable for however was faith. Despite the reality of dwindling membership and no new signs of life in the fellowship for twenty years, they just *believed* God was going to do a new thing, and they were prepared to wait. They sold their failing premises to a housing association for £17,500 while they were waiting, and continued to meet for worship in each others homes. Tetley's Brewery were also waiting, but waiting to auction The Furnival Public House as it was no longer viable. The old pub went up for auction in the spring of 1996 and the famous four went along with their URC Minister, Duncan Wilson, and the Methodist Superintendent John Vincent - and bought it for £49,500! As Bishop Peter Price had advocated, this was pitching a tent among the confused majority. The local people resisted at first, getting a petition of 300 signatories in their attempt to stop 'their' pub, becoming a church. In the meantime others were listening to God - and responding. Peter Hurley, who had been preparing for priesthood, left seminary and came to live locally; Una Burke, who had been in religious life for 30 years, working with disengaged young people, came to live in the area; Helen Platt, who had come to a consciousness of God through Yoga and who was studying at the Urban Theology Unit, felt drawn to the area, and a Baptist Minister Jane Grinonneau felt a strong call to the area too. With the support of Baptist and Methodist Home Mission and the prayers and gifts of hundreds of people, The Furnival was opened 'under new management' in September 1996. The Membership soon grew to nine, and is now eighteen. For the first six months we did little but *listen* - listen to the local people expressing their needs and concerns; listen to others working in the area. From the listening an agenda of issues was compiled – God's agenda for the transformation of individual and community. 46% of all families with children were lone parent households - facilities for parents and children were wanted. 19% of residents suffered chronic ill-health or disability, they wanted somewhere to go; people wanted a meeting place and an eating place. Many expressed concern for the children disengaged from mainstream education and on the street day and night. Above all people expressed a real longing for skills and for work (only 24% of the potential workforce in employment). No bank, nor launderette in the area, high crime, much of it driven by the drug scene - this was the place where God was doing a new thing. The Furnival has become an LEP (we describe it as an LEA - Local Ecumenical Adventure). We are Constituted as Baptist Methodists, URC, but now have Roman Catholic, Anglican and post denominational members too! Since 1996 £O.5 million has been raised to create a Community Cafe and Lunch Club, an informal education project for disengaged young people (in the old cellar); more recently, redundant retail outlets have been 'given' by the City Council to a new community owned company, to provide a launderette, nearly new clothes and re-furbished furniture. Plans are at an advanced stage to access more vacant property and use it for workshops, and a healthy living centre. All these essential facilities will provide opportunities for skills development and increase employability. Some 150 people come through the premises each week - but above all else we see the Kingdom come, as injustice and oppression are confronted. Once a month we meet as Furnival People, and explore what is God doing here, and what is our part as co-creators. Amazing things have happened - endless stories of pain and joy which beg interpretation in the light of God-with us. Mission needs to be redefined, as Me, Incarnating, Spent, Staying, Inserted, Open and Naïve. This way we believe we simply become the hands and feet in the Way of Christ through which God does far more than we could ever ask or imagine. Many significant partnerships have developed across all the key service providers; what we do we must do together, above all we must continue to listen faithfully, and listen with the heart, with non-judgemental loving, continuing to amplify the voice of the silent and help the blossoming of the urban wilderness.

* * * * * * * * * * * *

The video 'A day in the life of Josie' followed this presentation, which concentrated on the life of a woman who had spent time in prison, had come to the Furnival 'to scoff' and been drawn into Christian faith and baptism by its ministry and was now a helper in the drop-in centre. We were shown a shot of a nun, member of the community, who said, wisely, that the longer she stayed the less she said, because 'I realise that I know nothing'; and of a friend of Josie on her post-Christian phase of life, who agreed that she was basically the same person, if different, but that whereas once she had 'listened with her head, now she listened with her heart'.

Case study (2)
Awakening to Christ's way of relating
Revd Julia Dowling (Luton)

An Industrial Town in the South; a mini Asia in England. "Underneath it all they are just like us". This was a comment made by a member of Beech Hill Methodist Church during a discussion about our neighbours. This comment might not mean very much until you realise who our neighbours are. Our neighbours are mainly Asian Muslims from Pakistan, Bangladesh, Kashmir and India. There are some Irish, Afro-Caribbean and English also still living in an area of 20,000 people. We are situated in the Bury Park area of Luton, just to the west of the main town centre and on the main route from Dunstable. The people live in terraced streets of small houses with Luton football ground in the middle.

Luton itself is a town of 220,000 with a well known airport and the Vauxhall Car factory. Overall 59% of the population are members of ethnic minorities.

Bury Park has a foreign feel to it, with most of the shops belonging to Pakistani or Indian shop-keepers, who sell jewellery, clothing, groceries; Halal butchers and hot foods from their countries of origin. The main garment worn by both men and women is the Shalwar Kameez, national costume of Pakistan and made famous when Princess Diana and Jemima Khan were photographed wearing it.

Within half a mile there are: 6 Mosques, 2 Hindi temples, 5 Churches of various denominations, a SikhGudwari, an Orthodox Synagogue, the Quaker Friends' house, and the Bahai and Zoroastrians who meet in local houses. The majority faith is Islam. However the Muslims from different ethnic areas have their own mosques and disagreements between them often spill over into the community.

The whole place has an air of vibrant decay. Vibrant because it is a microcosm of many other places in Britain where different cultures and faiths gather to live and work. Existing alongside the colourful variety of dress and language is the ever present tension of people who are wary of 'the stranger' from another land. Decay is due to the air of general neglect that pervades the place. Unemployment is high, especially amongst Asian and Afro-

Caribbean men. The birth rate is high. Housing is largely private rented. Small shops and businesses have sprung up among the houses, adding to the general feeling of untidiness.

Education is offered through the four Primary schools and a Comprehensive. Of the primary schools two are all Asian, one has a few Caucasians and the other is 70% Asian. The comprehensive is 65% Asian.

Beech Hill Methodist Church

Comprising 77 members who come from a wide radius; some having moved out to seek better housing and schooling for their children, others who have not the means or the will to leave the area live locally.

Several years ago the church had sunk to a very low state. They felt besieged and threatened by the Asians who were fast taking over the area and turning it into a mini Pakistan. There was a feeling of 'what's the point in keeping a church in a Muslim area'. This led to a decline in relationships between those in the church. This feeling of isolation and fragmentation was compounded by the lack of understanding shown by the minister and other churches in the Circuit and by a leadership that could only see one option - closure of the church. However, there were a few people who strongly believed that there must be a way forward that did not include 'pulling out' of the area. These people pushed for a different solution.

Grassroots, an ecumenical organisation offered to put a 'Mission Partner' from Brazil in to work part-time at the church. This was funded by the Mission division of Methodism and the Circuit. For the church, it was as if a light had suddenly been turned on and, although it only glowed dimly, its glow was to get brighter and bigger as the years went by. At last, someone was interested in them, listened to them and worked with them to try to discover where God was in the church and the area.

Then during this time, after a year with no minister of their own but being caretakered by a young minister, the church started to work together and a way forward seemed to be emerging. With the arrival of a new minister with inter-faith experience there began to be real hope and there was no longer talk of closing but of re-building - re-building the fellowship, the worship, the relationships with the community.

The church decided on a policy of non evangelisation. Rather, we value the diverse faith communities that surround us. A survey undertaken by the church found that the community had four main needs: health and education, leisure and entertainment, youth work and violence awareness. Our task now is to see how we can help the community to provide in these areas.

As a minister I have never worked in an area where God matters so much; some 90% of the community are believers although it is rarely a Christian faith. None the less, faith is important and very evident on a daily basis.

The church's wish is to engage with others of all faiths and none to enable all of us to seek God's will for our area. A 'Why?' Group discusses the important questions of life and has recently commenced a study of contextual Liberation Theology. The aim is to help people to see what has liberated them and what might further that liberation for others. This throws up all the usual social, political and justice problems encountered by those who live in a depressed area with people mainly from other countries who have to cope with officialdom.

Bible study does not play a central role in the church; people having been put off in the past by the didacticism of their youth, although they enjoy discussion groups. Worship does however give prominence to Biblical teaching alongside contextual understanding for today. This enables us to link past and present seeking to find resources to meet the apparent needs of Christians to engage and other faiths to be taken seriously.

One of the major difficulties is the patriarchal nature of Pakistani culture; this pervades the area and women do not attend the mosque. It can be inhibiting but there are ways of working within it.

There is much hope as we struggle to find our task and tackle it realistically as well as spiritually.

VI

Junction or Terminus?
Christianity in the West at the Dawn of the Third Millennium

David Smith

At the beginning of this century the writer Arnold Bennett published a novel with the title *Anna of the Five Towns*. The story concerns a young woman who seeks, without success, to experience religious conversion in the context of traditional Methodist revivalism. Bennett describes how, in a desperate search for a personal experience of God, Anna attends evangelistic meetings only to find that the preacher's appeals leave her cold and unsatisfied. In a passage which probably reflects his own alienation from the Evangelical religion of his parents, Bennett depicts Anna trying to imagine what it might be like to be converted, or to be in the process of being converted:

> *"She could not. She could only sit, moveless, dull and abject... In what did conversion consist? Was it to say the words 'I believe'? She repeated to herself softly 'I believe, I believe'. But nothing happened. Of course she believed. She had never doubted or dreamed of doubting, that Jesus died on the cross to save her soul, her soul, from eternal damnation..... What then was lacking? What was belief? What was faith?"* [1]

Bennett's novel was published in 1902 and it contained an implicit warning that traditional Protestant religion was losing contact with a changing culture. However, this warning went largely unheeded; chapels were still well filled and although a few children of believers might, like Anna, go the way of the world, it remained possible to suppose that well-tried methods of evangelism were adequate to secure a continuing harvest of converts. Indeed, by the end of the first decade of this century the delegates to the great missionary conference in Edinburgh in 1910 could speak with confidence of 'the evangelisation of the world in this generation'.

From our vantage point, nearly one-hundred years after Bennett wrote the words just quoted it now seems clear that, with the sensitive antenna of a great artist, he had correctly detected the

---

1   Arnold Bennett *Anna of the Five Towns* (London; Methuen;1925), p.71

condition of the British churches even before the cataclysm of 1914-1918 changed the world for ever. The problem for the churches today is no longer how to respond to a relatively minor slippage in relation to the children of the chapels, *the chapels themselves have gone, or are in the process of going.* The stark reality of the situation facing institutional Christianity at the present time is expressed in the haunting words of a poem entitled 'The Chapel' by the Welsh writer R. S. Thomas. The poem describes the isolated and ugly nonconformist building which had once been ablaze with revival fires but now simply settles 'a little deeper into the grass'. The closing lines recall the religion of those whose amens once rang out from the building, people who were 'narrow but saved; In a way that men are not now'[2]

Many theologians and sociologists now warn us that the crisis confronting institutional religion in the Western world is one of truly massive proportions. Here is David Mills, an American Episcopalian, who uses almost apocalyptic language to describe the plight of Anglicanism: not only has the fat lady sung "but the cleaners have left, the security guards have turned out the lights and locked the doors, and the wrecking ball waits outside for tomorrow's demolition work. But even so, a few men and women in purple shirts .... still huddle together in the now dark stalls, chatting excitedly of all the great operas they are going to stage"[3]. This prediction of ecclesiastical meltdown is endorsed by the New Zealander, Michael Riddell who says bluntly in a recent book: "The Christian church is dying in the West". Believers, reacting as bereaved people often do to a great loss, may deny this reality, bolstered by 'small outbreaks of life', yet it is beyond doubt, says Riddell, that Christianity in the West is afflicted by a terminal sickness.[4]

Now it might be argued that the experience of Christians within the Evangelical tradition does not match this kind of gloomy

---

2   R. S. Thomas, *Selected Poems* (London, J.M Dent, 1996), p.81. Thomas's work constantly explores the interface between faith and modernity and wrestles with the problem of doubt. See also *No Truce With the Furies* (Newcastle-upon-Tyne; Bloodaxe Books, 1995)

3   I regret that the source of this quotation has been misplaced. It was included in an analysis of Anglicanism circulated by the REFORM Group within the Church of England.

4   Michael Riddell, *Threshold of the Future*: *Reforming the Church in the Post-Christian West* (London; SPCK, 1998), p.1.

diagnosis. It may be the case that mainline denominational religion is facing crisis, but an Evangelicalism enlivened by the fires of charismatic renewal can point to empirical evidence that contradicts the generally negative assessment of religion in the West. The success of the Alpha Course, the surge of new churches in many parts of Britain, the growth of the Spring Harvest event, or the rise in 'born again' religion in the United States, are all indications that a robust Evangelicalism seems to be immune from the trends toward decline and secularisation afflicting more traditional forms of institutional Christianity. Or so the argument goes.

I am afraid I view such claims with considerable scepticism. The late Klaas Bockmuehl, himself an Evangelical and a shrewd and wise observer of contemporary cultural trends, said that Christians in general had given very little thought to the challenges posed by secularisation and he noted that Evangelicals were often content "if they add to their numbers even when the overall state of Christianity deteriorates".[5] In fact, the born-again phenomenon in America suggests that it is possible for very considerable numbers of people to profess conversion without such a movement resulting in any significant change in the surrounding culture. In the words of the American theologian, David Wells,

> "The vast growth in evangelically-minded people in the 1960s, 1970s and 1980s should by now have revolutionized American culture. With a third of American adults now claiming to have experienced spiritual rebirth, a powerful countercurrent of morality growing out of an alternative worldview should have been unleashed in factories, offices and board rooms, in the media, universities and professions.... But as it turns out, all this swelling of evangelical ranks has passed unnoticed in the culture.... The presence of evangelicals in American culture has barely caused a ripple"[6]

The reason for this I suggest, is that American Evangelicalism no longer possesses an alternative worldview to that which operates at the heart of Western culture. At the beginning of the 1960s the sociologist of religion, Peter Berger, argued that American churches had become prosperous precisely because they provided religious support and sanction for the secular values

---

5 Klaas Bockmuehl, `Secularization and Secularism – Some Christian Considerations', *Evangelical Review of Theology*, 10/1, 1986 p.50-51
6 David Wells, *No Place for Truth* (Leicester; IVP, 1992), p.293

87

which dominate everyday work and life in society. In a striking passage Berger observed that a child growing up in a suburban, churchgoing family in modern America bore "an uncanny resemblance to the young Buddha whose parents shielded him from any sight involving human suffering or death". In such a situation, Berger said, the prophets or poets who point to "the darkness surrounding our clean little toy villages" are regarded as "candidates for psychotherapy"[7].

I suggest that the fundamental question Evangelicals must consider concerns the core beliefs and values which define this tradition. Has the term 'evangelical' been gutted of its original meaning? Has it become a mere slogan, divorced from the truths and values derived from the gospel of Jesus Christ? Is it the case, as David Wells claims, that Evangelicals are among those who are on the easiest of terms with the modern world and so have lost their capacity for dissent?

This may seem a harsh and negative judgement, but it compels us to ask whether there are grounds for hope that Christianity might be capable of transforming and renewing modern culture? What is the concrete evidence which might suggest that the churches of the West can discover the spiritual and intellectual strength required to challenge the fundamental values of a deeply secular society? With regard to the Evangelical movement, is it conceivable that this tradition might have resources that would enable it to resist the monstrous idols which extend their control into every aspect of our economic and social life? And can we really believe that it might be capable of offering the world at the dawn of the third millennium a radically new and hopeful vision of human existence, shaped by beliefs and values that would lay the foundation for a culture characterised by love, compassion, justice and life lived within limits? I suggest that it would be a bold person who answered these questions affirmatively. On the basis of present evidence we might as easily anticipate that churches will survive in Europe only through an increasing syncretism with Western culture which requires them to abandon the possibility of ever again being a force able to transform the world for the glory of God.

---

7   Peter Berger, *The Noise of Solemn Assemblies* (New York; Doubleday, 1961), p.48

Protestant Christianity has been deeply committed to cross-cultural mission throughout the modern period with the result that the faith of Christ has been successfully transmitted and translated into hundreds of cultures around the globe. Indeed, this has resulted in one of the major transformations of our times in which Christianity has become a world faith with its heartlands no longer in Europe or North America but in those regions of the world once identified as 'mission fields'. Two hundred years ago William Carey and his colleagues were determined to ensure that churches resulting from the cross-cultural transmission of the Christian faith should take recognisably Indian form. Their insistence that the gospel should be *contextualised*, that Indian believers should be encouraged to express both the form and the content of their faith in ways that were clearly Asian, led to tensions between the missionaries and their supporters in Britain. Few Christians today would deny the wisdom and validity of Carey's approach to mission and it is generally recognised that (to quote the Lausanne Covenant) churches should be "deeply rooted in Christ and closely related to their culture".[8]

However, while assent may easily be obtained for this principle when it relates to churches in other cultures overseas, the issue becomes problematic and painful when we ask the question: *to which culture do our churches relate?* Or, to put the issue another way, can there be a valid contextualisation of the gospel for Western culture at a point at which that culture is passing through dramatic and far-reaching change? The problem with the chapels described in the poem with which we began is precisely that they seem to belong to another age, to a world that has passed away. William Storrar, describing the challenges faced by the Church of Scotland, suggests that our cultural context is one in which people are "bewildered by shifting patterns of family and household living, short-term and part-time unemployment, the global media and information highways... seven day shopping in cathedral-like shopping malls... and a myriad of other cultural trends'. In this situation, he says, "the local parish kirk can seem as anachronistic

---

8   The phrase is from chapter 10 of the Lausanne Covenant. See J.D. Douglas (ed), *Let the Earth Hear His Voice* (Minneapolis; Worldwide Publications, 1974), p.6

as the traditional high street grocer's shop, the Edwardian music hall or the nationalised coal mine, a relic of another age".[9]

I think in this connection of the church in which I grew up and was nourished in the Christian faith. The building in which we worshipped was erected in the 1880s and was called the Baptist Tabernacle, although anything less like a tabernacle would be difficult to imagine. It was certainly not intended to be portable, a movable sanctuary for a pilgrim people. On the contrary, those who built this enduring tabernacle were not moving anywhere; they had just arrived as respected and valued members of bourgeois society. Today this listed building is overlooked by a massive shopping mall and as consumers pour into the 'Harlequin Centre' every Sunday it is just possible that they may glance at this striking example of our national religious heritage. This building, like so many others, erected in an earlier time to the glory of God, has become a huge obstacle to mission in a postmodern world. Stranded at the edge of a car park serving the consumerist temple which now dominates the skyline, the Tabernacle symbolizes the immobility of the church and its captivity to cultural forms perceived as outmoded and irrelevant.

I suggest that the challenge which this cultural context presents to Christian mission is one of the greatest and the most dangerous ever to have faced the church. On the one hand, it should be possible for churches possessing two centuries of accumulated experience and expertise in cross-cultural missionary endeavour to discover faithful and creative ways of ensuring that Christ becomes a living option for a generation shaped by postmodern culture. This is the concern of people like Dave Tomlinson, John Drane and William Storrar who argue that Christianity in the Western world has been so closely wedded to the culture of modernity that "it is being left behind by the pace of change, and is finding it increasingly difficult to be taken seriously by the new, emerging mainstream Western culture".[10]

---

9   William Storrar's comments were made in a lecture delivered at the University of Aberdeen and published by the Divinity Department. He has developed the theme further in a special issue of the journal *Theology in Scotland* devoted to an analysis of the subject of 'The Future of the Kirk'. See Occasional Paper 2, March 1977.

10   The quotation is from John Drane, *Faith in a Changing Culture* (London; Marshall Pickering, 1997), p.44. The reference to Dave Tomlinson relates to his controversial proposals in *The Post-Evangelical* (London; SPCK, 1995). The issue

On the other hand, while a fearful retreat to the ghetto is not an option for faithful Christians, no-one should underestimate the daunting nature of the missionary challenge presented by the Western world today. Frankly, I worry about Christians who treat postmodern culture on very easy terms as though it were a neutral context likely to prove immediately hospitable to the message of Christ. On the contrary, the West increasingly takes on the appearance of a vast cultural swamp which threatens those who wander into it, without due regard to its dangers, with suffocation and death. The Christian mission has never been a merely human enterprise and those who have struggled to bring Christ into the heart of another culture know well the pain and the perils of this task. Those Christians who rightly take the need to relate the Gospel to the changing culture of the modern West seriously, must also pay attention to the history of mission if they are to avoid being sucked into the bog of a materialist and relativistic worldview. Perhaps it must also be said that, assuming a re-evangelisation of Europe is possible, this cannot be achieved by an evangelistic quick fix employing new technologies; rather it is likely to be a work of generations, perhaps even centuries.

Surveying the long history of the Christian movement, Andrew Walls observes that it reveals that local and regional churches can wane as well as rise: "Areas where Paul and Peter and John saw mighty encouragement are now Christian deserts. The Christian heartlands of one age can disappear within another".[11] The church in Jerusalem provided the first launching pad for cross-cultural mission, yet it was quickly eclipsed by a new centre of dynamic spiritual life and, retreating to a monocultural expression of the faith, it rapidly became marginal to the purposes of the Holy Spirit. The history of the cross-cultural transmission of faith warns us that no particular local tradition of Christianity is guaranteed survival. The same Christ who declared that the gates of hell cannot prevail against his church, warned local churches in Asia Minor that he would remove their candlesticks and terminate their existence if they ignored his call to repentance. The conclusion is unavoidable: if Christianity in the West loses contact with the gospel and

---

is also discussed in detail in David Hillborn's *Picking Up the Pieces: Can Evangelicalism Adapt to Contemporary Culture?* (London Hodder & Stoughton, 1977).

11   Andrew Walls, `Christian Expansion and the Condition of Western Culture' in *Changing The World* (Bromley, Kent; MARC Europe, n.d) p.14. This is a quite brilliant discussion of this subject.

becomes blind to its captivity within a secular culture then it will be found to be suffering a sickness unto death. In fact, the perplexity experienced by many European Christians today is related to the struggle to come to terms with the fact that the real centres of Christian life and growth are now located in the non-Western world. Long established habits of thought and practice based on the assumption that the churches of the West occupy centre-stage in the purposes of God must be abandoned in the light of this new reality. We now find ourselves standing in the wings, witnessing others take the lead in God's still unfolding drama of redemption. Believers in the southern hemisphere are well aware of this change and often enquire whether we really understand its significance. For example, the Chinese theologian Choan-Seng Song has asked a series of question of us: What will the future of Christianity be in the West? How will believers in Europe "recapture the power of the gospel"? And how will they "relate to Christians in the Third World who will surpass them in numerical strength?"[12]

It would not be an exaggeration to say that a fundamental concern of the great prophets of Israel was to challenge the complacency and pride which resulted from a distorted understanding of divine election and to warn the chosen people that they, no less than the surrounding nations, would experience God's judgement if they continued to violate the conditions of the covenant. Consider, for example, the bombshell dropped in Jerusalem by Isaiah at the start of his prophecy. He addresses the self-confident citizens of a place regarded as holy and indestructible as "you people of Gomorrah" and declares that God could not bear their "evil assemblies" since they concealed godless lives and hard hearts beneath a cloak of religious respectability. (Isaiah 1: 10-1 7). Much later, when the judgement has fallen, Ezekiel has to confront the insane optimism of people who still live with the illusion that the troubles are temporary and will soon be over. To the exiles who refused to accept reality and tried to comfort each other with the assurance that everything would quickly return to normal, Ezekiel is told to say simply: "The end has come! The end has come!" (Ezekiel 7: 1).

---

12 Choan Seng-Song, *The Compassionate God* (London; SCM Press, 1982), p.7

The same kind of language is found on the lips of Jesus. Standing in the prophetic tradition he cuts through the facade of religious pretence and warns his hearers that neither centuries of tradition, nor strict adherence to the external duties of religion, can provide protection against the Living God who demands of those who profess to know him love and obedience. Nor are such warnings directed only to the religious establishment. Jesus tells his most intimate circle of followers that. whenever a religious tradition becomes lifeless and powerless then, however hallowed and loved it might be, the end is near. "If the salt loses its saltiness... it is no longer good for anything, except to be thrown out and trampled by men" (Matt. 5:13). At the end of the New Testament we hear the glorified Christ uttering exactly the same warnings to Christian congregations beginning to settle down in the world and making their peace with the dominant culture of Rome. The church at Ephesus, for example, brought to birth a generation earlier in what might be called the fires of revival, is called to repentance and told that it faces a terminus: "If you do not repent, I will come and remove your lampstand from its place" (Rev.2:5).

There is one passage in the New Testament which, it seems to me, speaks to Western Christianity today with peculiar power and relevance. In the letter to the Romans, Paul wrestles with the mystery of the purposes of God in human history and, in particular, the problem of the relationship between fallen Israel and the Gentile church. The language used suggests that Paul realises, even at this early stage in Christian history, that age-old tendencies toward religious pride and an unlovely arrogance toward other people were surfacing among non-Jewish believers. In a text that has received less attention than should have been the case, Paul says to the Gentile church: "Do not be arrogant, but be afraid.... Consider the kindness and sternness of God: sternness to those who fell, but kindness to you, *provided that you continue in his kindness*" (Rom. 11: 17-24).

Where then does this leave us? Are we at a junction or a terminus? Is Christianity in the Western world beyond hope, beyond genuine renewal? Viewed from certain angles the crisis we face seems to be of such huge proportions that none of the remedies offered in the past promise a solution. Michael Riddell, speaking about New Zealand, says, "I have lost count of the number of revivalist movements which have swept through my homeland promising a massive influx to the church in their wake. A year after they have faded, the plight of the Christian community seems largely unchanged, apart from a few more who have grown cynical through the abuse of their goodwill, energy and money."[13]

However, the Christian faith bears a message of hope and the God worshipped through Jesus is astonishingly patient, kind and gracious. Jonah had a second chance to respond to this missionary God by recognising the radically new thing that Yahweh was about to do beyond the confines of the elect; Peter had three opportunities to withdraw his protest note against the disturbance caused to his religious world by the missionary priorities of the risen Christ. Moreover, the biblical texts mentioned earlier suggest that in the mercy of God, endings are followed by new beginnings. Beyond the agonies of loss and exile, Israel hears the word of the Lord which says "Forget the former things... See I am doing a new thing" (Isaiah: 43:18-19). At the point at which the people of God finally accepted that there was no way back to things as they had been, they were able to receive the divine revelation of something radically new. Is this perhaps the situation in which we find ourselves today? The long era of Western Christendom is over and we live amid the remnants of that period, trying to make sense of our situation and confused and disoriented by the complexity of the changes occuring both in society and in the church. Yet even as we grieve over the fragmented and weakened condition of the churches, can we begin to catch the indications that God is inviting us to participate in something new?

In 1978 Malcolm Muggeridge delivered two lectures at the University of Waterloo in Canada under the title 'The End of Christendom... But Not of Christ'. The lectures were full of the wit and wisdom that made Muggeridge such a superb communicator and his concluding statement is worth quoting:

> *"It is precisely when every earthly hope has been explored and found wanting, when every recourse this world offers, moral as well as material, has been explored to no effect, when in the shivering cold the last faggot has been thrown on the fire and in the gathering darkness every glimmer of light has finally flickered out, it's then that Christ's hand reaches out sure and firm. .... So, in finding in*

---

13   Ridell, op.cit, p.14

everything only deception and nothingness, the soul is constrained to have recourse to God himself and to rest content with him".[14]

These words offer hope to individuals floundering in a collapsing culture; but what if we replace Muggeridge's reference to the individual soul and apply his analysis instead to the church? Might it not be that the present stage of transition and deep uncertainty concerning Western Christianity provides a providential opportunity for believers to rediscover Christ and the gospel and, in the light of this, to find quite new ways of being the church today? There is a growing body of opinion across all denominational boundaries that the present crisis does indeed offer an unprecedented opportunity to rediscover the true nature of the Christian church and to return to first principles. Might we go even further and suggest that with the collapse of what was regarded as 'Christian civilization' we may also recover *what it actually means to be Christian?* Jacques Ellul once said that "Christendom astutely abolished Christianity by making us all Christians" and he went on to claim that in such a culture 'there is not the slightest idea what Christianity is".[15] The concern to distinguish between 'real' Christianity and its counterfeits in various types of culture-religion has been a central feature of the Evangelical movement, which suggests that this tradition could yet play an important role in what David Bosch called the 'emerging ecumenical paradigm'.

What is striking is that the context within which this new model of mission is taking shape is one in which more and more voices are heard outside the church expressing their own laments at the condition of the culture of the West. For example, Michael Ignatieff, in a preface for the programme for the 1999 BBC Promenade Concerts notes that works like Beethoven's Choral Symphony and Mahler's 'Resurrection' Symphony are expressions of the faith of their composers in what he calls the modern myth of the Ascent of Man - the belief in human progress as the powers of reason were brought to bear "against the forces of ignorance and the cruelty of fate". And yet, Ignatieff, confesses, "we are no longer certain that we can believe such stories". The barbarism around us seems to make nonsense of the claim that our species is marching along a path toward

---

14 Malcolm Muggeridge, *The End of Christendom* (Grand Rapids; Eerdmans, 1980), p.56
15 Jacques Ellul, *The Subversion of Christianity* (Grand Rapids; Eerdmans, 1986), p.36

civilisation, with the result that "it is easy to feel that (in hearing these works) we are listening to the music of our lost hopes and illusions, reaching us like the last light from extinguished stars".[16]

Is it perhaps the case that our collective experience of life in a far country, with as much distance between us and the hated father as possible, is mirrored here? And might it be that we are approaching a point at which the prodigal "comes to himself" and begins to devise strategies of return? In 1994 a conference took place on the Island of Capri at which some of Europe's leading philosophers met to discuss the subject of religion. Their conclusions were published in a book edited by Jacques Derrida and Gianni Vattimo. According to Vattimo, "the dissolution of the great systems that accompanied the development of science, technology and modern social organization'- in other words, *the end of modernity* - has created a situation in which philosophy must once again give serious and prolonged attention to the subject of religion. European societies, he says, are faced with a situation in which there is a widespread fear "of losing the meaning of existence, of that true and profound boredom which seems inevitably to accompany consumerism". Using language that seems to echo the parable of the Prodigal Son, Vattimo says that at this precise point in history something we thought "irrevocably forgotten is made present again....... the repressed returns" and... in the current resurgence of religion we seem to hear "a voice that we are sure we have heard before".[17] Is this the prodigal beginning to come to himself ?

If so, then as the secular myths that provided the foundation for the project of the Enlightenment lose their credibility in the light of bitter historical experience, so Christians must come to terms with the end of the era in which their faith and practice was shaped by its long assimilation with Western culture. The point has been well made by the Canadian theologian, Douglas John Hall,

> "... the Christian movement can have a very significant future - a responsible future that will be both faithful to the original vision of this movement and of immense service to our beleaguered world. But to have that future, we Christians must stop trying to have the kind of

---

16 Michael Ignatieff, 'The Ascent of Man' *BBC Proms Programme* (London; BBC Publications, 1999), p.8

17 Jacques Derrida and Gianni Vattimo (eds), *Religion* (Cambridge; Polity Press, 1988), p.80

future that nearly sixteen centuries of official Christianity in the Western world has conditioned us to covet". [18]

Recently it has been suggested that the present experience of Christians in the West is similar to that of people in traditional societies in Africa when passing through rites of initiation which enable them to move from one status to another. Victor Turner used the word *liminality* to describe the experience by which, for example, a young boy is separated from his mother and isolated in a camp outside the village where he will be prepared for entering manhood. He then finds himself in a liminal stage in which the old identity has been lost and the new one is not yet conferred. This is a confusing and frightening experience and the first instinct is to return to the familiar status, to go home and regain the comforting relationship with his mother! And yet this liminal stage is a necessary precondition for growth, it is the passage through which boys become men and discover new status with fresh responsibilities and new opportunities in life. Just so, the churches of the West seem to be in a liminal state; the old is dying and must be left behind, but it remains entirely unclear from our perspective just what we shall become. Driven to the margins of our culture, reduced in status and dignity, our instincts, like the initiate in the African village, is to cling to the old and the familiar and to maintain structures and patterns of life that have been established for centuries. But, as Alan Roxburgh points out, however uncomfortable this liminal stage may be, it contains the potential for transformation: "The decisions that are made in this phase shape the future of the group" and for the churches, liminality brings the possibility of rediscovering what it truly means to be the pilgrim people of God. [19]

Perhaps then this liminal stage through which the churches of the West are passing offers us an opportunity for a theological and spiritual renewal beyond our ability to visualise at present. If so, we shall certainly need to listen to sisters and brothers from the southern hemisphere who already offer us valuable critical perspectives precisely because they speak from a vantage point

18 Douglas John Hall, *The End of Christendom and the Future of Christianity* (Leominster; Gracewing Publications, 1997), p.ix

19 See Alan J. Roxburgh, *The Missionary Congregation, Leadership and Liminality* (Harrisburg, Penn; Trinity Press International, 1997), p.33.   Victor Turner's discussion of the concept of the 'liminal' is in his *The Ritual Process: Structure and Antistructure* (New York; Aldine DeGruyter, 1969).

outside the culture of the West. Indeed, this is one of our key resources today and, whatever the problems of our times, we have an unprecedented opportunity to grasp something more of the dimensions of the unfathomable love of Christ "together with all the saints" (Eph.3:18-19).

A revised version of this material is included in a forthcoming book from Paternoster Press under the title *Crying in the Wilderness.*

VII

POST-MODERN MISSION

A PARADIGM SHIFT IN DAVID BOSCH'S THEOLOGY OF MISSION?

Kirsteen Kim

In his renowned *Transforming Mission*,[1] David Bosch delineates what he calls "the postmodern paradigm" (349) for mission. Magnificent in its clarity, scope and depth, the book has understandably fulfilled Lesslie Newbigin's prediction that it would become "the indispensable foundation for the teaching of missiology for many years to come" (back cover). However, without doubting its value and usefulness for teaching missiology, this paper questions, in some important respects, Bosch's claim that his missiology is post-modern.

The weakness of Bosch's "emerging ecumenical consensus" on mission was apparent in its very year of publication - 1991 - when the Seventh Assembly of the World Council of Churches at Canberra famously failed to find a consensus.[2] The Assembly took a pneumatological theme with a missionary thrust based on a creation theology, "Come, Holy Spirit - Renew the Whole Creation". Canberra was particularly influenced by the work of the Justice, Peace and the Integrity of Creation "process" (JPIC) - which evidenced at Canberra particular concern for feminism, ecology, and indigenous spirituality - and the "Spirit of life" theology of Jürgen Moltmann.[3]

---

1   David J. Bosch, *Transforming Mission: Paradigm Shifts in Theology of Mission* (Maryknoll: Orbis, 1991). Page references in brackets are to this book.
2   Michael Kinnamon (ed), *Signs of the Spirit: The Official Report of the Seventh Assembly of the World Council of Churches, Canberra Australia, 7-20 February 1991* (Geneva: WCC, 1991).
3   Moltmann's book *The Spirit of Life: A Universal Affirmation* (London: SCM) was published in English in 1992. His contribution to the Canberra theme, "The Scope of Renewal in the Spirit" was published in 1990 in Emilio Castro (comp.), *To the Wind of God's Spirit* (Geneva: WCC). In this connection it is interesting to note that though Bosch refers to Jürgen Moltmann's work at least twenty times this is only to works published in the 1960s and 70s and, with one exception (see note 22), not to his pneumatology.

In his chapter outlining post-modernity, Bosch recognises its eco-feminist dimensions when he notes briefly that it involves a "basic reorientation":

> One should, again, see oneself as a child of Mother Earth and as sister and brother to other human beings. One should think holistically, rather than analytically, emphasize togetherness rather than distance, break through the dualism of mind and body, subject and object, and emphasize 'symbiosis' (355).

He suggests "profound and far-reaching consequences" of such a change of worldview for the epistemology of mission but these are not worked out in his book. Creation theology and its attendant concerns at Canberra are hardly mentioned in *Transforming Mission*. As far as *feminism* is concerned, though he does allude to women, nowhere does Bosch mention feminism as a theological or philosophical movement.[4] Bosch hardly touches on *ecology* or on the perceived global environmental crisis which fuelled the JPIC process.[5] Thirdly, the related interest in *"indigenous spiritualities"* or "the spiritualities of indigenous people" is missed.[6] This lack of interest is surprising in view of Bosch's own direct experience of indigenous peoples during his formative years as a missionary in Transkei (1957-71).[7]

---

4   Bosch does set the record straight regarding the involvement of women in modern mission (328) and pleads for their representation as part of the recognition of the "apostolate of the laity" (470-2). He also includes a discussion of Paul's attitude to women (151-52) from which it would seem that his own position is not unlike the Apostle's: Paul's preoccupation with the relationship of Jews and Greeks almost excludes the slaves and freepersons, male and female of Gal 3:28 (151).

5   In a short monograph published posthumously, Bosch mentions ecology as a topic with which a missiology of Western culture must deal but it is not included in his ingredients "of crucial importance". David J. Bosch, *Believing in the Future: Toward a Missiology of Western Culture* (Leominster: Gracewing, 1995), 55-56.

6   In fact, in an article reflecting on the conference, Bosch questions why the life of indigenous peoples should be addressed in connection with ecology at all. David Bosch, "Your Will Be Done? Critical Reflections on San Antonio", *Missionalia* 17 (2 Aug, 1989), 126-38.

7   Bosch, an Afrikaner, has been criticised for lack of engagement with the religious experience of black Africans. See Frans J. Verstraelen, "Africa in David Bosch's Missiology: Survey and Appraisal" in Willem Saayman & Klippies Kritzinger (eds), *Mission in Bold Humility: David Bosch's Work Considered* (Maryknoll: Orbis, 1996); T.A. Mofokeng, "Mission Theology from an African Perspective: A Dialogue with David Bosch" in J.N.J. Kritzinger & Willem Saayman (eds), *Mission in Creative Tension: A Dialogue with David Bosch* (Pretoria: S.A. Missiological Society, 1990). Cf. J. Kevin Livingston, "The Legacy of David Bosch", *IBMR* 23/1 (Jan 1999), 28.

By its very nature, *Transforming Mission* is retrospective; it documents what has been already been resolved not the debates of today.[8] In that sense it was inevitably already out of date by the time of its publication. However, its lack of reference to these contemporary issues is remarkable when we consider that Bosch was a section leader at the San Antonio meeting of the Council for World Mission and Evangelism of the WCC at which the influence of JPIC was clearly evident. Though preparation of his book was in its final stages in 1989, Bosch does refer to the San Antonio meeting six times (389, 429, 460-61, 467, 487, 489) but never with reference to JPIC themes. When he concludes that San Antonio contained no new missiological reflections,[9] it is hard to avoid the conclusion that what falls outside his paradigm has simply been ignored.

The Spirit of mission

The fact that Bosch passes over feminism, ecology and indigenous spiritualities raises the question of whether Bosch's paradigm can be described as a truly post-modern one, even by his own criteria above. In the light of Canberra, it reveals both Bosch's lack of a creation theology and suggests also the limited nature of his pneumatology.

Bosch has been praised for his emphasis on the work of the Holy Spirit in mission.[10] In highlighting the Orthodox contribution to theology of mission and the theology of Luke, Bosch draws attention to *the Spirit of mission* (especially 113-115, 516-517). In various places he cites with approval the seminal work of such as Roland Allen (four times) and Harry Boer[11] (five times) in mission pneumatology. He uses the title of John V. Taylor's seminal *The Go-Between God* (378),[12] but chooses to ignore the thrust of Taylor's work, which is toward a Spirit at work in the whole creation, in the achievements of human culture, and in all

8   Cf. Robert J. Schreiter, "Transforming Mission", Review Article, *IBMR* 15/4 (Oct 1991), 181.
9   David Bosch, "Your Will Be Done? Critical Reflections on San Antonio", *Missionalia* 17 (2 Aug, 1989), pp126-38.
10 See, for example, Wilbert R. Shenk, "The Mission Dynamic" in Saayman & Kritzinger, *Mission in Bold Humility*, 89.
11 Harry R. Boer, *Pentecost and Missions* (Grand Rapids: Eerdmans, 1961).
12 John V. Taylor, *The Go-Between God: The Holy Spirit and the Christian Mission* (London: SCM, 1972).

relationships.[13] Bosch is keen to emphasise the missionary nature of the Spirit but he stops short of discussing *the mission of the Spirit*, which was the subject of Canberra. Despite his best efforts, Bosch has what William Burrows has called a "Jesusological pneumatology" in which the Spirit is an "afterthought used to explain God's activity in the church in connection with Jesus, ignoring the mystery of the Spirit as an equal modality or *persona* of the divine nature".[14]

The mission of the Spirit

Debate at Canberra "concentrated on the issue of the action of the Spirit within and outside the church, and on the criteria necessary to recognise the presence of the Spirit".[15] In the later part of his book, Bosch does allow for the wider work of the Spirit in the world and is prepared to be surprised by the Spirit (379, 489, 494. See also 150, 517). He comes close to the language of Canberra when he writes, "[Mission] is mediating the presence of God the Spirit, who blows where he wishes, without us knowing whence he comes and whither he goes (Jn 3:8)[16]. Mission is 'the expression of the life of the Holy Spirit who has been set no limits'[17]" (494). However, the broader pneumatology implied here cannot easily be integrated with earlier parts of the book, particularly the biblical foundations which owe their origin to his doctoral studies on Christology and the Kingdom in the 1950s.[18]

---

13 Taylor states at the outset that "the Spirit who is central to Paul's theology is the same being whom the Old Testament knew as the Spirit, or Breath, of God" (Taylor, *The Go-Between God*, 6 - a statement he justifies in his second chapter, 25-41), and argues on this basis for a broad understanding of mission in keeping with the activity of the "Creator Spirit" (Taylor, *The Go-Between God*, 38). Harry Boer has also more recently pleaded, taking Allen as his starting point, for an integration of creation and redemption in evangelical missionary theology. Harry R. Boer, "The Holy Spirit and Church Growth" in Wilbert R. Shenk (ed), *Exploring Church Growth - a Symposium* (Grand Rapids: Eerdmans, 1983), 249-259.

14 William R. Burrows, "A Seventh Paradigm? Catholics and Radical Inculturation" in Saayman & Kritzinger, *Mission in Bold Humility*, 129. Burrows argues that this is because Bosch missed a seventh paradigm, "a Catholic Inculturation Paradigm" (122.), which emerged only at Vatican II and is "marked by a *radical vision of what is entailed in interfaith and cross-cultural dialogue that leads to the contextualization and inculturation of Christianity*" (130f - italics original).

15 Emilio Castro, Editorial, *ER* 43/2 (April 1991), 163.

16 A text frequently used at Canberra and quoted by Bosch here but strangely absent from his scripture index.

17 Bosch gives the source of this quotation as G. Rosenkranz who attributes it to G. van der Leeuw.

18 Bosch's doctoral work was on the teaching of Jesus on the Gentile mission under Oscar Cullmann. See David J. Bosch, *Die Heidenmission in der Zukunftsschau*

102

Despite his promotion of *missio Dei*, the structure of his book reveals that Bosch bases his "ecumenical paradigm" firmly on the historical activity of the second person of the Trinity and on the church. His lack of attention to the "Old Testament"[19] and to John's gospel[20] means he does not develop a creation missiology. He does not link the Spirit which descended on Jesus Christ and was poured out at Pentecost with the "breath" or "wind" of God in the Old Testament, therefore the mission of the Spirit is bound very closely to the missionary activity of the church. Thus, when Bosch seeks to broaden mission to take account of the "comprehensive" nature of salvation, he can do so only by increasing the scope of the church's missionary activity (393-400). Hence mission still appears as a *work* to be achieved by organisation and strategy. In this sense, his "post-modern" paradigm is very much in the mould of the Enlightenment project[21] and the possibilities raised by *missio Dei* for deriving mission from the very nature of God are not fully realised.[22]

A corollary of Bosch's close association of the Spirit with the church is the uncontextual nature of his missiology. The "hermeneutics of suspicion" brought to the attention of the church by feminist and liberation theologies has cast grave doubt on the validity of a global theology. Jan van Butselaar has argued, in the light of Canberra, for the need of a contextual approach to theologising - "thinking locally, acting globally",[23] but Bosch

---

Jesu: Eine Untersuchung zur Eschatologie der Synoptischen Evangelien (Zurich: Zwingli Verlag, 1959). Verstraelen notes that, by Bosch's own admission, his theology developed in the 1960s and has not essentially changed since then. Verstraelen, "Africa in David Bosch's Missiology", 10.

19 The OT is dealt with in less than five pages (16-20). In the new paradigm, pride of place and by far the most attention is given to "Mission as the Church-With-Others" (368-389). The other "elements" are also activities of the church.

20 Bosch considers the mission theology of Matthew, Luke and Paul. Cf. Philip H. Towner "Paradigms Lost: Mission to the *Kosmos* in John and in David Bosch's Biblical Models of Mission", *Evangelical Quarterly*, 67/2 (1995), 99-119.

21 Cf. Schreiter, who finds the post-modern paradigm for mission less convincing than the others: "It looks more like an extension or fulfilment of the Enlightenment paradigm than any new one". Schreiter, "Transforming Mission", 181.

22 From his section on *missio Dei* (389-393), it appears that Bosch's reaction to the use of the concept to by-pass the church in mission prevents him from fully embracing the idea of the mission of the Spirit "that includes the church" (390 - a quotation from Jürgen Moltmann, *The Church in the Power of the Spirit* (London: SCM, 1977), 64) and indeed rejecting the pneumatalogical definition of mission that he finds in, for example, *Gaudium et Spes* (391).

23 Jan van Butselaar, "'Thinking Locally, Acting Globally': The Ecumenical Movement in the New Era", *IRM* LXXXI/323 (July 1992), 363-373.

follows the traditional ecumenical approach of thinking globally and applying this locally.[24] What is more, Bosch's hope is in the institutional church in its Western form of which he is part, despite its legacy of "missionary war", holocaust and apartheid. He looks for another Pentecost that will transform it into the outgoing community of equals it was intended to be (384-9). The source of that wind of the Spirit will be from within, from the Bible and Christian tradition, as the outline of *Transforming Mission* makes clear. The use of extra-biblical and extra-ecclesial sources from contextual experience is not contemplated.

In his discussion of mission as dialogue, Bosch acknowledges the role of the Spirit in other faiths in *preparatio evangelica* (484)[25] but he hesitates to give any value to the faiths themselves. Bosch's approach of "bold humility" which recognises an "unresolved tension" - "We cannot point to any other way of salvation than Jesus Christ; at the same time we cannot set limits to the saving power of God" - has been highly acclaimed.[26] Whereas this "abiding paradox of asserting both ultimate commitment to one's own religion and genuine openness to another's" (483) is undoubtedly a step forward in theology of religions, shelving the issue until the *parousia* (489) may be criticised as unrealistic in the context of pluralism and as not taking our responsibilities of discernment seriously as those who claim to have the Spirit of Christ. In the post-modern world and in the life of faith we are called to live with uncertainty but perhaps this uncertainty should be discussed not in relation to the question of *whether* the Holy Spirit is active in others' experience but in relation to *where* and *how* the Spirit is active there.[27]

Though the Canberra documents are, on the whole, cautious about identifying the Spirit's work outside the church, it is clear that there was substantial pressure at Canberra to do so. Despite its reticence, the creation theology of JPIC pointed to a broader understanding of the work of the Spirit than the Western missionary movement has allowed. This meant that contextual

---

24 Cf. Saayman, "A South African Perspective...", 50-51; Verstraelen, "Africa in David Bosch's Missiology", 12-14; Mofokeng, "Mission Theology from an African Perspective", 173-5.

25 Citing the work of D.T. Niles, Max Warren, and Kenneth Cragg.

26 Cf. the title of Saayman and Kritzinger, *Mission in Bold Humility*.

27 Cf. Stanley J. Samartha, "The Holy Spirit and People of Other Faiths", in Castro, *To the Wind of God's Spirit*, 59.

theologising had to be recognised. The Holy Spirit did not only accompany the Western missionary, the Spirit was immanent in the field. It also strongly implied that the Spirit was active not merely "among" but *in* the faith of those of other religious orientations, especially indigenous spiritualities.

The Spirit and spirits

This approach might be taken as another example of the liberal tendency to unite all faiths, in this case by making them all responses to one Spirit, if Canberra had not also held the seeds of a different approach. At the same time as broadening the work of the Spirit, discussion at Canberra also began to break down the monopoly the Holy Spirit has held in the West by talking in terms - albeit vague - of many spirits in this world, thus setting the Spirit in a pluralistic context. This development was prompted by what became the most talked-about aspect of the Canberra Assembly, Prof. Chung Hyun Kyung's provocative plenary presentation.[28] Somewhat superficially, Chung employed the spirit-language of Korean shamanism to inspire feminist action to bring about the renewal of creation.[29] Although Chung called on other spirits, she rather romantically identified them with the Holy Spirit, and thus justified the widespread accusations of syncretism. Chung's presentation was significant not so much for its content as for the ensuing discussion of the relationship of the Holy Spirit with what were termed "the spirits of the world" becoming the focus of debate.[30] Thus a truly pluralistic theology of spirits was glimpsed in which a variety of spirits interact and interpenetrate one another.

Bosch's work, as most contemporary Western Christian theology, conceives of only one spirit - the Holy Spirit. Similarly post-Enlightenment philosophy, influenced most notably in this area by Hegel, has recognised only the spirit of the West. However the experience of the twentieth century has been of the reality and durability of other spirits and the dangers of all totalitarianism. Furthermore, the rise of pentecostal/charismatic

---

28 Chung Hyun Kyung, "Come Holy Spirit - Renew the Whole Creation" in Kinnamon, *Signs of the Spirit*, 37-47.
29 Her theological approach is spelt out in Chung Hyun Kyung, "Ecology, Feminism and African and Asian Spirituality: Towards a Spirituality of Eco-Feminism" in David G. Hallman (ed), *Ecotheology: Voices from South and North* (Geneva: WCC, 1994), 175-178.
30 Kinnamon, "Canberra 1991: A Personal Overview and Introduction" in Kinnamon, *Signs of the Spirit*, 15.

movements, with their interest in exorcism and spiritual warfare, and of New Age spiritualities, which borrow from indigenous spiritualities, is associated with post-modernity (and formed an important part of the background of Canberra). Both these movements recognise in some sense the "excluded middle" of cosmic forces which have been disregarded, even eliminated, by the scientific mind-set of modernity.[31] It could be argued that to be truly post-modern, the Holy Spirit must be couched in the pluralistic context of a multiplicity of spirits. This very kind of pluralistic spirit-language began to emerge in the debates at Canberra.

At the same time the reality of other spirits seemed to be in some doubt since it was found necessary in the Canberra documents to refer to them in quotation marks.[32] The ease with which Chung summoned "spirits" (clearly demythologised in her theology[33]) alarmed those participants for whom spirits were a supernatural reality.[34] In "Pluralism and the Problem of the Discernment of Spirits", a pre-Canberra article which was prophetic of the debate, Justin Ukpong discussed the use of Spirit and spirits in the Bible, pointing out that spirits are both good and evil entities.[35] He applied the biblical language of Spirit and spirits to three contemporary pluralistic contexts - radically secular ideologies, other religions, and the Christian community.[36] The potential of the spirit-language of Canberra lies in its use by groups which conceived of "spirits" differently and invested them with varied levels of reality, and therefore in its wide applicability.

---

31 Paul G. Hiebert, "The Flaw of the Excluded Middle", *Missiology* 10/1 (Jan 1982), 35-47. Cf. Aloysius Pieris, *An Asian Theology of Liberation* (Maryknoll: Orbis, 1990), 71-74.

32 For example, p15, p112, p254. The "Reflections of Orthodox Participants" referred to "a 'private' spirit, the spirit of the world or other spirits" as the subjects of debate at Canberra (Kinnamon, *Signs of the Spirit*, 281).

33 See Chung Hyun Kyung, "'Han-pu-ri': Doing Theology from a Korean Women's Perspective", *ER* 40 (Jan 1988).

34 Robeck reports one Pentecostal saying to him after Chung's presentation, "I was so afraid I sat shaking through the entire presentation, pleading the blood and interceding in tongues". Robeck, "A Pentecostal Reflects...", in Bong Rin Ro & Bruce J. Nicholls (eds), *Beyond Canberra: Evangelical Responses to Contemporary Ecumenical Issues* (Oxford: Regnum, 1993), 112. See also Raymond Fung, "The Spirit World", in Ro & Nicholls, *Beyond Canberra*, 60-3.

35 Justin S. Ukpong, "Pluralism and the Problem of the Discernment of Spirits", *ER* 41/3 (July 1989), 418-20

36 Ukpong, "Pluralism and the Problem...", 421-24.

This theology of Spirit and spirits made discernment of spirits an urgent necessity. In his very helpful article, Ukpong had laid the biblical foundations for this, taking 1 Corinthians 12.10 as his starting point. Here discernment is a charism of the Holy Spirit for "recognizing the genuineness of inspirations", "taking right decisions in accordance with God's will", and "recognizing God's action in the world at large".[37] The Orthodox expressed "alarm" at Chung's lack of discernment and insisted that pneumatology must not be separated from Christology and the doctrine of the Trinity.[38] The report of Canberra pointed out that "[The Holy Spirit] is distinct from other 'spirits' in this world, whether benign or demonic".[39] Two criteria for discerning the Spirit were suggested: (i) the Holy Spirit "points to the cross and resurrection and witnesses to the Lordship of Christ"; and (ii) the biblical list of the fruits of the Spirit.[40] Thus Ukpong's article and the discussion at Canberra suggest a theology which could link the Spirit of creation firmly with the Spirit of Christ - at least in Christian belief - and at the same time make room for other "spirits". These may be discerned, in a way described in the Christian Scriptures, as either co-operative or unco-operative with the Christian mission without having to be co-opted or subsumed into Christianity. Those of other persuasions could, just as legitimately, claim ultimacy for another "spirit".

In actual practice, it was clear that discernment of spirits was an area fraught with difficulty, as the discussions at Canberra on the Gulf War demonstrated. These difficulties were compounded by the power question of who defines the criteria for discerning the Spirit.[41] As Saayman has pointed out, Bosch's espousal of "bold humility" is a sign that he speaks as a representative of a group that is conscious of being powerful.[42] His is a theology from above not from a context of minority status or oppression. Bosch's Holy

---

37 Ukpong, "Pluralism and the Problem...", 417. While bearing a similar title and also thoroughly surveying the biblical material, Eduard Schweizer's "On Distinguishing Between Spirits" (*ER* 41/3 (July 1989), 406-415) concludes that everywhere in the New Testament the Spirit is linked to Jesus and states a conservative position that links the Spirit so closely with Christ that even the "breath" or "wind" of God must be distinguished from the Holy Spirit.

38 "Reflections of Orthodox Participants", 279-282.

39 "The Report of the Seventh Assembly", para 81, Kinnamon, *Signs of the Spirit*, 254.

40 "The Report of the Seventh Assembly", para 93, Kinnamon, *Signs of the Spirit*, 256.

41 Castro, Editorial, 163. Chung argued that it was time Third World women had a go at discernment instead of Western male theologians - Kinnamon, "Canberra 1991", 16.

42 Saayman, "A South African Perspective...", 50-1.

Spirit is not free from its splendid isolation to interact with the other spirits of a pluralistic world. The Canberra documents frequently stress the free and unbound nature of the Spirit (often alluding to John 3.8), which may suggest that a pneumatology for the twenty-first century needs to begin from the experience of spirits below rather than from the assertion of one Spirit from above.

Conclusion

Bosch's work represents a considerable achievement, it has been rightly acclaimed, and remains indispensable but, as Bosch himself points out, no paradigm is the last word in missiology (511). It may be that in retrospect Bosch's work will be seen not as setting out a new paradigm but as summarising the old. In the words of Robert Schreiter, *Transforming Mission* "tells us where we have come in mission at the end of the twentieth century".[43] This is no mean achievement but in view of (a) his lack of attention to essential post-modern issues - feminism, ecology and indigenous spiritualities, and (b) the church-centredness of his pneumatology, it must be questioned whether Bosch's paradigm is as post-modern as he claims and therefore whether his missiology is appropriate for the twenty-first century. The post-modern paradigm will take into account not only the Spirit of mission but also the mission of the Spirit, a mission which takes place in the context of other spirits. In any truly missionary encounter, these spirits need to be recognised and their natures discerned by the Spirit of Christ.

---

43   Schreiter, "Transforming Mission", 181.

REPLYING TO GOD'S INVITATION:

an agenda for Mission Studies in Britain and Ireland after the 1999 BIAMS Conference, "An Invitation to God's Future"

Philip Thomas

Within days of leaving Oxford I travelled to Africa. It presented a disturbing contrast. The fifth residential conference of the British and Irish Association for Mission Studies offered four days to contemplate the dynamic possibilities in God's future. As only an occasional visitor to the African continent, the next month made it difficult to avoid the overwhelming question of whether for most of the world there was any future worth looking forward to at all?

Of course the contrast was not absolute. I do know enough about Africa to realise that the social, political and environmental problems are not the only things that a Western observer needs to notice. In terms of Christian history especially, there are many more hopeful signs to be explored. Equally, the conference itself did not limit itself to a merely theoretical approach to eschatology. As the principal speaker, Jürgen Moltmann is well known for his ability to conjure a vision of the future which is almost tangible, but the programme was designed to allow Theo Sundermeier to bring a missiological test to that vision and for Anton Wessels to add a critique in terms of European cultural history. Crucially too, case studies of mission on the margins of English society grounded all the talk in the practicalities of church life, and the discussion process – organised around the interest areas of participants – succeeded in bringing concrete experiences and issues into the development of the Conference theme. Notes from those discussions are appended to this essay, which is primarily intended to outline the sort of work that students of Christian mission may need to undertake over the next two years before the next Conference in 2001. But before that, some attention must be given to the way in which that work might be undertaken, and the direction and purpose that it should have.

A testing agenda

My own personal agenda after the conference was clarified from an unexpected source. Caught somewhere in that tension between eschatological theory and apocalyptic reality, I found myself reading Freya Stark's autobiography.[1] A great traveller and map-maker throughout Europe and the Middle East, she was uniquely positioned to comment on the gathering storm-clouds of the second world-war. She likened the situation to "the feeling of theatre, where the audience knows the tragedy of which the stage is unaware". The power of tragedy is in bringing to life things which are normally in the background, behind the scenes, the amorphous unanswered questions which we forget or take for granted because the spotlight is on the narrow foreground of ourselves. "And suddenly those vast outlines are shifting: the vagueness that we had taken for solid landscape is moving down upon us .... The essence of tragedy – the sudden irruption of the background of life into the small, well-ordered, tender and fragile gardens of men."

At the same time Stark was also involved in a fierce correspondence with her publisher, who wanted her to 'soften', to romanticise, a manuscript from her travel journals. They were not written for a literary public, she insisted, or the fashions of the day. "... I can never remember a time when I have not tried to write for the century which follows rather than for the one in which I live. This is not because I feel my writing is exceptionally good, but because Time is a reality for me. I feel things in movement proceeding into their future from their past; and my immortality is of no personal interest, for I feel it – for instance – when I rescue some place-name and put it safe on the map out of oblivion, to be seen by many who can never know my part in its existence there."

Pathetically perhaps, this humanistic vision of 'Time as a reality' helped settle my misgivings. Christians dare to believe that our spasmodic forays into the unknown territory of justice and truth are also marked indelibly on the map of God's purposes. I was actually glad of the need to test ideas from a mission studies conference in a situation where the credibility of Christian mission is not just an academic question.

Not that ideas are unimportant. Vision and mission go together. What we think worth working for is determined to a large

---

1   *The Coast of Incense: Autobiography 1933-39,* (London, 1953) pp269-275

extent by what we believe can be ultimately achieved. Hope and endurance are linked in a biblical view of a suffering universe (Romans 5:3ff). And this is not just a matter of pious expectation. During the conference prospects for the future were being eagerly measured throughout the country. Tabloid journalists delved into supposed prophecies of Nostradamus; Wimbledon fortnight in England produced the annual attack of Henmania; while in Northern Ireland desperate negotiations attempted to keep the bright hopes of the Good Friday peace agreement alive. Speculation – optimism – politicking - all these very human preoccupations have their eschatological equivalents within church communities - but an invitation to God's future lies elsewhere. As Christopher Rowland who gave the opening address will have it, apocalyptic is not only about the ultimate vindication of God's purposes, it is also "unmasking ... the true character of contemporary society and the superhuman forces at work in opposition to God's righteousness in the world".[2] Mission studies involve the task of unmasking, of making plain the amorphous unspoken questions, which are so often taken for granted by the church because the spotlight is focused so narrowly on the foreground of its own survival.

The theory of practice, and the practice of theory.

I began autobiographically on purpose. A notable feature at Oxford was the way theory and practice came together. The significant way in which the case studies from Luton and Sheffield engaged with the lectures of Moltmann and Sundermeier has already been noted.. In the concluding plenary Howard Mellor, Principal of Cliff College, identified this as a niche which BIAMS could usefully fill. Tim Yates in the Newsletter highlighted "bringing together of missionary thinkers and practitioners ... the discernment of what mission means in the contemporary world in thought word and deed" as the strength of the organisation and the conference[3]. Parig Digan, a member of the executive, has for years urged his Columban colleagues to see the missiological academy and the missionary frontier as belonging on the same planet![4] I offer my own low-key 'case study' and superficial reflection on it as an indication of how these hopeful aspirations could be furthered.

---

2   *Radical Christianity: a Reading of Recovery,* (Oxford, 1988) p75
3   *BIAMS Occasional Newsletter 13* (September 1999) p3
4   *BIAMS '99 in Oxford: a Columban Reflection* (July 1999)

It is apparent that BIAMS cannot and should not attempt to oversee any magisterial research project like North Atlantic Mission Project, or co-ordinate academic goals of British and Irish teaching institutions in the manner of the Selly Oak or Mill Hill colleges or the Kimmage Mission Institute. Neither will it be tempted to duplicate the production of programmes, publications or specialised ministries in the manner of individual mission agencies or orders. What it can do is keep alive the background questions of theology and culture for missionary activists, and attempt to keep theoreticians honest by insisting that real missiological questions are confronted in their research, rather than preoccupations dictated by the latest funding proposal.

This role involves more than just bringing academics and practitioners together. It is not just proximity that is required, but engagement. The conference method could be refined, but, essentially, placing appropriate biblical and theological study alongside descriptions of the goals and practices of particular pieces of missionary work, almost creates its own dynamic. What is necessary is space for mutual questioning. Academics do not stand in judgement on a practitioner, but equally their work is not dismissed out of hand by those labouring on the front-lines of mission. Criticism may be directed in both directions, but the perceived goal must be creative. "Good missiology" said Professor Werner Ustorf of Birmingham University during the concluding plenary panel discussion, "should help the church occupy places of risk. Naming the dangers of judgement and salvation can secure the practitioners as they seek to address them." He viewed progress in this direction as the most positive outcome of the conference where, as he saw it, "BIAMS came of age".

Relocating the centre.
Mission studies in Britain and Ireland are burgeoning at the moment, although the overall shape of the discipline is not clearly defined. Planning for a day-conference on curriculum development, BIAMS was able to identify 150 different institutions where mission or evangelism courses were taught. Many of these were requirements for ordination or bible-training qualifications, tackled with varying degrees of enthusiasm or commitment depending upon the ethos and perceived purpose of the bodies concerned. Others were included as components within pastoral or practical theology modules, but increasingly the

centrality of mission is being recognised in the training and educational provision of churches and educational bodies. Cranmer Hall, Durham, undertook a serious review of a whole curriculum centred on mission themes; Cliff College offers graduate and post-graduate courses in various areas of mission and evangelism; clusters of doctoral research projects are organised from Edinburgh, Birmingham and Leeds. The Department of Mission at Birmingham University (drawing especially on staff and students in the Selly Oak colleges) is one of the largest centres for teaching and research in the University, while groups of scholars stimulated by the Oxford Centre for Mission Studies, and the programmes initiated from the Henry Martyn Centre in Cambridge are building towards a critical mass of academic discourse. Less formally the concerns developed by bodies like the Gospel and Our Culture movement - now taking renewed institutional form under the aegis of the Bible Society - reflect a growing determination among Christians generally to locate mission within the setting of western culture. The expressed interests of BIAMS members also reflect this awareness.

The variety of situations in which mission studies are carried out give promise of lively debate, but the diversity of approaches which are brought to the discussion means that communication is not easily established. The development of academic centres for the study of mission in Britain and Ireland is fairly recent. Typically the task has been carried out on the margins of church life, and among those who are enthusiasts for the cause of world mission. As a result there is no agreed procedure or method. For some it has to do with a virtually utilitarian acquisition of skills, for others a detached observation on the fringe of historical or cultural studies. It is probably true that most missiological research in these islands has been based on historical and archival material, but increasingly the need for biblical and theological synthesis is being recognised.

This expansion of the scope of British and Irish mission studies is to a large extent a recognition of the post-Christian character of life in these islands. Traditionally it might be imagined that mission was something done by "us" to "them" a long way from home! No longer is this possible. The churches here find themselves actually at the frontier of contemporary mission, and as such the role of mission studies becomes much more central to reflection on the life of Christian discipleship today. A leading figure in the renaissance of missiological study in Britain, Andrew Walls, has spoken of the task of "subverting the curriculum". In this he is not just talking about documentation within the theological academy, but part of a process by which the whole church reconceptualises its nature and its task.[5] He sees this as a project which must be theological, ecumenical, international and co-operative. At the heart of the process is theological integration - "inserting the shape of the church as it is today on to intellectual and theological maps that were drawn according to the canons of what used to be". But this is not just something to be performed by academic theologians alone. Almost by definition, mission has to do with the world, the secular and profane, the matter of fact. Walls insists, "Mission studies must interact with ongoing work in the history, languages, political, economic and social organization, cultures, and literature of the Southern continents (not to mention many aspects of the Northern). Therein are some of the twentieth-century equivalents of Assyrian inscriptions and demotic Greek papyri with the potential to reorder much sacred and much profane learning." The study of mission is presented as an essential element in the renewing of Christian theology: in what has become virtually a cliché, we are turning from theologies of mission towards missionary theology. It is time to turn the words into actions. These actions moreover will take place within the world of scholarship, but mission being what it is, equally outside places of formal learning within a setting of challenge and response, the clash of values and cultures, and attempts to bring comfort and hope to the ineluctable burden of human need.

It is from the variety of skills and experience that members of BIAMS bring together that some engagement with that task should be possible. Members will have their own personal commitments to action or study, but in coming together there is opportunity to move forward the integrative and renewing task that Andrew Walls has outlined. In a magisterial survey of mission studies Kirsteen Kim, Secretary of BIAMS, has identified various intellectual, theological and spiritual "interfaces" where mission studies have a formidable and formative role to play.[6] Missiologists have important marks to make on the map-work of their areas of

5   Andrew F.Walls "Structural Problems in Mission Studies" in *The Missionary Movement in Christian History: Studies in the Transmission of Faith (1996) p150ff.*

6   Kirsteen Kim, "Mission Studies in Britain and Ireland: Introduction to a World-Wide Web", forthcoming in *The British Journal of Theological Education.*

expertise, but at times they also need to raise their vision to plot the journey which their map makes possible.

For BIAMS to concentrate on creating in its own programme a discourse of 'practice-theory' (the two elements coming together in almost Germanic compound terminology – until there is a better way of expressing it) could determine both the methodology and the agenda for on-going study on the wider front of missionary and theological studies throughout the region. It has already been suggested that special interest groups should concentrate on case-studies which provoke and address substantial missiological questions. Day and residential conferences have been planned at which the actual position of the churches and Christian belief in Britain and Ireland will form the context for reflection and learning. The questions themselves should be clarified and analysed from the differing standpoints of participants. Understanding will be increased, and further action stimulated.

The Shape of the future.
Given an appreciation of the apocalyptic, the eschatological dimension of the mission of God which so inspired the Oxford Conference, few will fall into the trap of confusing the progress of the church's mission with the glory yet to be revealed. Yet the intensity of the church's struggle in the west and the powerful counter-forces which it confronts throughout the world, means that a grasp of the history and theology of mission is an irreplaceable source of steadiness and resolve for Christians in their calling.

That other map-maker, Freya Stark, struggling with the notebooks in her lifelong home in Tuscany, reflected on "the foolish noise of Fascism" arising about her in much loved places. Her recollection went back to the descendents of the Celts, Goths, Visigoths, Huns, Franks and Lombards who had passed that way before her. Her hopes did not falter. "The young country had even then been old, and had taken them, century after century, wave after wave, to her heart, torn with violence and blood: and the wounds had healed and the conquerors had forgotten to conquer …. There they had blossomed, in saints, in scientists, in painters, mechanics, architects, in all that makes life noble and easy, in all that we have ever wished for in this world to live for and not to die."[7]

---

7   *Op.cit.,* p275

We who in our own day hear foolish sounds - poverty, oppression, racism, apathy - will claim no less a hope. Understanding the promise to patriarchs, prophets, poets, and apostles, and even the frail bearers now of over 2000 years of obedience to the missionary vision we will also be steadied in our resolve to make simple marks, placed on antique maps, which can still show travellers the way ahead in safety.

So What Was the Point?
Reflections During and After the BIAMS Conference
John D'Arcy May

It is when tensions begin to develop and manifest themselves as animosities that one can usually tell when a broad discussion such as the one we had at Oxford is beginning to touch the 'neuralgic point' that is really at issue. My working group's 'pointer to the future' was: "Our missionary priority should henceforth be, no longer 'our' witnessing to 'them', but we and others witnessing together". Presenting this proposition, I was immediately challenged: "Witnessing to whom or what?". Understandable as it is coming from people who have invested much in costly witness to the Gospel in difficult situations, this response pinpoints the difference we were - mostly unconsciously! - trying to formulate, the newness of the emerging missionary situation. This obtains not only among élites in the multicultural cities and societies of the West, which have their counterparts just about everywhere in today's world, but in rural areas and border regions which might once have been described as mono- or bicultural.

In all these situations we can no longer know definitively in advance what we are witnessing to until communication becomes two-way, until Sundermeier's *convivencia* has been established, because the convictions we will find we can share will emerge only out of a new relationship *diapraxis*. Here Werner Ustorf's warning - which seemed almost offensive to some - about the pernicious aspects of 'identity' thinking is apposite (those involved in Jewish-Christian-Muslim dialogue will have examples ready to hand!).

Dialogue, however, as communication-in-relationship, takes place at even deeper levels, where what is in the heart will communicate itself sometimes quite independently of the 'thought experiments' going on in the head. 'Authentic witness' will take place, in the end, when *cor ad cor loquitur* (Newman), when dialogue is 'centre-to-centre' (Aloysius Pieris) - not just from our (true) convictions to their (false) ones, but relationally. This, I submit, is how the witness at the heart of evangelisation is going to look in the global network of interreligious communication that is now coming into being.

Response to John May

Revd Dr Philip Thomas

I greatly appreciate your plea for "communication in relationship" and the need for "heart to heart" dialogue as an implication of Sundermeier's *Konvivenz* - and of Tim Yates' advocacy of the idea of *diapraxis* as it emerged from the recent IAMS consultation. I quite agree that this focuses on a crucial issue at the heart of the conference and indeed of mission studies as a whole. Dialogue, witness even, cannot be allowed to degenerate into what you so tellingly call "thought experiments".

Still, I think the insight needs to be explored further. Certainly heart to heart communication is part of the promise of God's future - "No longer need they teach one another to know the Lord..." but in the meantime isn't there still an element of provisionality, of being led patiently by the hand, about Christian discipleship? Communication needs to be tested. Faith is more than a matter of instinct. The knowledge of God and his ways is not self-evident to even the most sensitive observer. This, as Moltmann had it, is why we don't know anything without dialogue. It is in articulating faith ("believe in the heart... confess with the lips") that we discover its reality. As a young Indian woman once said to me in a confirmation class (about the only moment of excitement that I have ever managed to generate in a confirmation class I should say) when she had very tentatively recounted her own faith journey, '...well that's what I believe - and I didn't even know I believed it'!

Dialogue, a meeting of minds, an exploration of hopes and fears, is essential for our own integrity. At least - or perhaps at most - in authentic dialogue, we communicate that, "What is believed is held in good faith". But because any perception of God is "through a glass, darkly" it is inevitable that any attempt to express it in words is going to be incomplete. Dialogue will inevitably involve a measure of dialectic, of disputation. I believe it is important to recognise those points of difference as possible growth points for deeper understanding, as the matrix in which heart to heart communication can take place even when the meeting of minds is not conclusive.

This of course is where the issue of identity recurs.   I understand the dangers of tribalism, and recognise that Werner Ustorf's experience of post-war Germany makes him very sensitive to the dangers of identity thinking. But is it not possible to be identified with something without owning (in the sense of possessing) it, and to recognise that such an identity itself engages with a more comprehensive ontology? I may identify with my local football team - not a happy thought at the moment - but I plainly do not own it. Still, shouting on the terraces is how I participate in the otherwise abstract notion of "football". I can identify with the church while knowing that it is contingent upon the reign of the kingdom: I can identify with Christianity while seeing it as but an historical vehicle of the eschatological vision of God. So in the meantime my sporadic enthusiasm on the sidelines - feeble attempts to offer witness - what? to whom? - in the living contexts of human relationships and diverse social circumstances, I want to see as an anticipation of that "authentic mission" for which you so attractively appeal.

I am not sure how long I will want to hold to that sporting analogy - playing the game rather than merely observing it seems more in keeping with a missiological motif - but what I hope to see develop is a theology which holds together witness and dialogue, proclamation and the common good, identity and universality, uniqueness and pluralism, unity and diversity - in short, a foreshadowing of the vision of Ephesians, bringing to light the hidden purpose of God - a universe, all in heaven and earth, brought into unity in Christ. So when you ask "What was the point ... ?" my answer is that it was to diagnose more deeply the neuralgic discomfort that you have diagnosed so accurately rather than simply deadening its effect with some ecclesiastical painkiller. That way we may come to treat underlying problems rather than just get rid of the symptoms of the world's malaise. At least that is what I hope the conference was about, and what I hope the continuing BIAMS working groups will keep worrying away at over the next 18 months or so.

http://www.martynmission.cam.ac.uk/BIAMSConf.htm

18/10/99

INDEX